Experiencing Choral Music

BEGINNING

UNISON, 2-PART/3-PART

D1091851

Developed by

HAL•LEONARD® CORPORATION

McGraw Hill **Glencoe**

New York, New York   Columbus, Ohio   Chicago, Illinois   Peoria, Illinois   Woodland Hills, California

The portions of the National Standards for Music Education included here are reprinted from *National Standards for Arts Education* with permission from MENC–The National Association for Music Education. All rights reserved. Copyright © 1994 by MENC. The complete National Standards and additional materials relating to the Standards are available from MENC, 1806 Robert Fulton Drive, Reston, VA 20191 (telephone 800-336-3768).

A portion of the sales of this material goes to support music education programs through programs of MENC–The National Association for Music Education.

 **Glencoe**

The *McGraw-Hill* Companies

Printed in the United States of America.

Send all inquiries to:
Glencoe/McGraw-Hill
21600 Oxnard Street, Suite 500
Woodland Hills, CA 91367

ISBN 0-07-861104-0 (Student Edition)
ISBN 0-07-861105-9 (Teacher Wraparound Edition)

7 8 9   045   09 08 07

Credits

LEAD AUTHORS

Emily Crocker
Vice President of Choral Publications
Hal Leonard Corporation, Milwaukee, Wisconsin
Founder and Artistic Director, Milwaukee Children's Choir

Michael Jothen
Professor of Music, Program Director of Graduate Music Education
Chairperson of Music Education
Towson University, Towson, Maryland

Jan Juneau
Choral Director
Klein Collins High School
Spring, Texas

Henry H. Leck
Associate Professor and Director of Choral Activities
Butler University, Indianapolis, Indiana
Founder and Artistic Director, Indianapolis Children's Choir

Michael O'Hern
Choral Director
Lake Highlands High School
Richardson, Texas

Audrey Snyder
Composer
Eugene, Oregon

Mollie Tower
Coordinator of Choral and General Music, K-12, Retired
Austin, Texas

AUTHORS

Anne Denbow
Voice Instructor, Professional Singer/Actress
Director of Music, Holy Cross Episcopal Church
Simpsonville, South Carolina

Rollo A. Dilworth
Director of Choral Activities and Music
    Education
North Park University, Chicago, Illinois

Deidre Douglas
Choral Director
Aragon Middle School, Houston, Texas

Ruth E. Dwyer
Associate Director and Director of Education
Indianapolis Children's Choir
Indianapolis, Indiana

Norma Freeman
Choral Director
Saline High School, Saline, Michigan

Cynthia I. Gonzales
Music Theorist
Greenville, South Carolina

Michael Mendoza
Professor of Choral Activities
New Jersey State University
Trenton, New Jersey

Thomas Parente
Associate Professor
Westminster Choir College of Rider University
Princeton, New Jersey

Barry Talley
Director of Fine Arts and Choral Director
Deer Park ISD, Deer Park, Texas

CONTRIBUTING AUTHORS

Debbie Daniel
Choral Director, Webb Middle School
Garland, Texas

Roger Emerson
Composer/Arranger
Mount Shasta, California

Kari Gilbertson
Choral Director, Forest Meadow Junior High
Richardson, Texas

Tim McDonald
Creative Director, Music Theatre International
New York, New York

Christopher W. Peterson
Assistant Professor of Music Education (Choral)
University of Wisconsin-Milwaukee
Milwaukee, Wisconsin

Kirby Shaw
Composer/Arranger
Ashland, Oregon

Stephen Zegree
Professor of Music
Western Michigan State University
Kalamazoo, Michigan

EDITORIAL

Linda Rann
Senior Editor
Hal Leonard Corporation
Milwaukee, Wisconsin

Stacey Nordmeyer
Choral Editor
Hal Leonard Corporation
Milwaukee, Wisconsin

Table of Contents

Music & History

Choral Library

TO THE STUDENT

Welcome to choir!

By singing in the choir, you have chosen to be a part of an exciting and rewarding adventure. The benefits of being in choir are many. Basically, singing is fun. It provides an expressive way of sharing your feelings and emotions. Through choir, you will have friends that share a common interest with you. You will experience the joy of making beautiful music together. Choir provides the opportunity to develop your interpersonal skills. It takes teamwork and cooperation to sing together, and you must learn how to work with others. As you critique your individual and group performances, you can improve your ability to analyze and communicate your thoughts clearly.

Even if you do not pursue a music career, music can be an important part of your life. There are many avocational opportunities in music. **Avocational** means *not related to a job or career*. Singing as a hobby can provide you with personal enjoyment, enrich your life, and teach you life skills. Singing is something you can do for the rest of your life.

In this course, you will be presented with the basic skills of vocal production and music literacy. You will be exposed to songs from different cultures, songs in many different styles and languages, and songs from various historical periods. You will discover connections between music and the other arts. Guidelines for becoming a better singer and choir member include:

- Come to class prepared to learn.
- Respect the efforts of others.
- Work daily to improve your sight-singing skills.
- Sing expressively at all times.
- Have fun singing.

This book was written to provide you with a meaningful choral experience. Take advantage of the knowledge and opportunities offered here. Your exciting adventure of experiencing choral music is about to begin!

Lessons

Lessons for the Beginning of the Year

Lessons for Mid-Winter

Lessons for Concert/Festival

We Want To Sing

Composer: Roger Emerson
Text: Roger Emerson
Voicing: 2-Part

VOCABULARY

singing posture

stage presence

two-part music

rest

tie

 SPOTLIGHT

To learn more about posture, see page 11.

Focus

• Sing expressively.

• Perform two-part music.

Getting Started

Have you ever received a note or card from a friend that was so special to you that you kept it? When you have felt down, have you ever read the card again to lift your spirits? Singing has a way of making us feel good, too. "We Want To Sing" is an upbeat song with a positive message. Share this message with your audience through your enthusiasm, the excited expression on your face, and your **singing posture,** or *the way you stand when you sing.* These elements combined help to create your **stage presence,** or *your overall appearance on stage.*

◆ History and Culture

In the early 1970s while attending a choral camp in Shasta County, California, Roger Emerson, a small group of students, and a few counselors wrote "We Want To Sing." They wished to compose a piece of music that would reflect the message of goodwill to others and express the joy of singing.

"We Want To Sing" is an example of two-part music. **Two-part music** is *a type of music in which two different parts of music are sung together.* To make this song more interesting, the melody is sometimes found in Part I and other times found in Part II. As you learn "We Want To Sing," make sure that the melody line is clearly heard and not overshadowed by the other part.

Links to Learning

◆ **Vocal**

Establish your singing posture. Perform the following examples to practice singing in two parts.

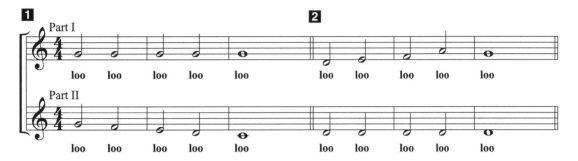

◆ **Theory**

In music notation, a **rest** is *a symbol used to indicate silence.* A **tie** is *a curved line used to connect two notes of the same pitch together in order to make one longer note.* Perform the following examples to practice rhythmic patterns with rests and ties.

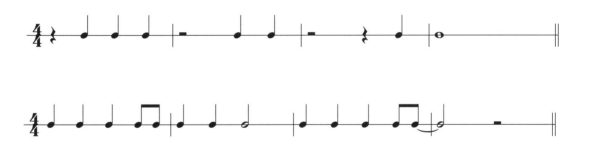

Evaluation

Demonstrate how well you have learned the skills and concepts featured in the lesson "We Want To Sing" by completing the following:

* Perform "We Want To Sing" expressively. In what ways did you show the meaning of the text through your overall stage presence?

* Select one person from Part I and one person from Part II to come forward and serve as listeners. As the choir sings measures 19–34, have the listeners decide if they can hear the two parts clearly, or if they hear one part overshadowed by the other.

We Want To Sing

For 2-Part and Piano

Words and Music by
ROGER EMERSON

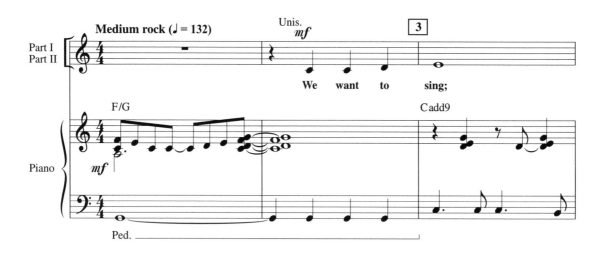

With our mus - ic_____ we can

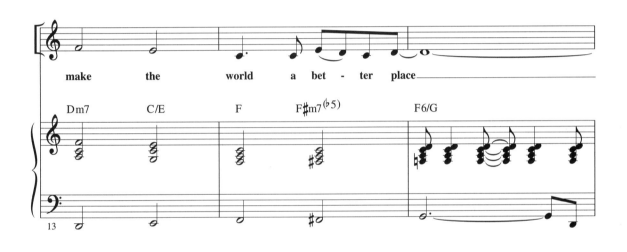

make the world a bet - ter place_____

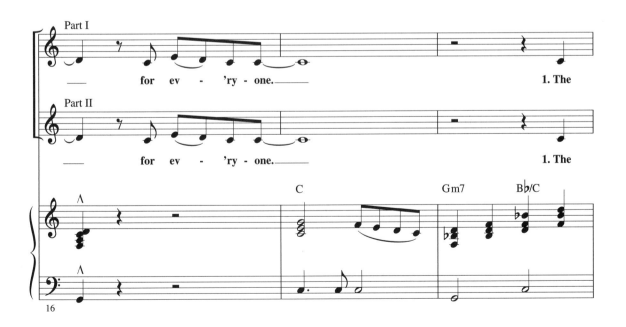

for ev - 'ry - one._____ 1. The

for ev - 'ry - one._____ 1. The

SPOTLIGHT

Posture

Posture is important for good singing. By having the body properly aligned, you are able to breath correctly so that you have sufficient breath support needed to sing more expressively and for longer periods of time.

To experience, explore and establish proper posture for singing, try the following:

Standing

- Pretend someone is gently pulling up on a thread attached to the top of your head.
- Let out all of your air like a deflating balloon.
- Raise your arms up over your head.
- Take in a deep breath as if you were sipping through a straw.
- Slowly lower your arms down to your sides.
- Let all your air out on a breathy "pah," keeping your chest high.
- Both feet on floor, shoulder-width apart.
- Chest high, shoulders relaxed.
- Neck relaxed, head straight.

Sitting

- Sit on the edge of a chair with your feet flat on the floor while keeping your chest lifted.
- Hold your music with one hand and turn pages with the other.
- Always hold the music up so you can easily see the director and your music.

My America

Composer: Based on "America," arranged by Joyce Eilers
Text: Samuel F. Smith, with new words by Joyce Eilers
Voicing: 2-Part

VOCABULARY

arrangement

descant

fermata

$\frac{3}{4}$ meter

 **SPOTLIGHT**

To learn more about vowels, see page 75.

Focus

- Read and perform music in $\frac{3}{4}$ meter.
- Relate music to other subjects.
- Perform music of American heritage.

Getting Started

What does America mean to you? What is your definition of patriotism? Patriotism can mean different things to different people. For some, it can be the image of the American flag or a historic monument. To others, it is the memory of those who have given their lives defending our country. Singing "My America" can help you express your feelings of patriotism and show what America means to you.

◆ History and Culture

The tune "My Country 'tis of Thee" can be found in many countries, including England, where it serves as the national anthem. In 1831, Samuel Smith, an American minister and author, wrote new words to this famous melody. It was first performed in Boston, Massachusetts, by a group of children at a Fourth of July celebration.

"My America" is an example of a choral arrangement. An **arrangement** is *a piece of music in which a composer takes an existing song and adds extra features or changes the song in some way.* Joyce Eilers has added new words and a **descant**, or *a special part that is usually sung higher than the other parts,* to the familiar tune "My Country 'tis of Thee" to create this arrangement.

Links to Learning

◆ Vocal

When singing in a choir, proper vowel sounds are the foundation of a good choral tone. Read and perform the following example to practice singing with uniform vowel sounds.

mee— may— mah— moh— moo   mee— may— mah— moh— moo

This symbol ⌢ is called a fermata. A **fermata** is *a symbol that instructs a musician to hold a note longer than its value.* Find a fermata in "My America."

◆ Theory

Read and perform the example below to practice reading rhythmic patterns in $\frac{3}{4}$ **meter,** *a time signature in which there are three beats per measure and the quarter note receives the beat.* Try conducting as you read.

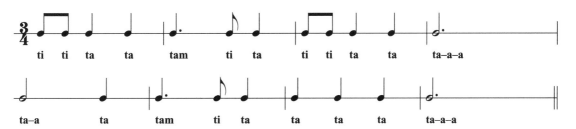

ti ti ta   ta   tam   ti ta   ti ti ta   ta   ta–a–a

ta–a   ta   tam   ti ta   ta   ta   ta   ta–a–a

◆ Artistic Expression

To develop artistry through writing, write an introduction to "My America" to be read at a performance. Choose words appropriate to the patriotic style of this piece that will encourage your listeners to think of what America means to them.

Evaluation

Demonstrate how well you have learned the skills and concepts featured in the lesson "My America" by completing the following:

- Sing and conduct measures 5–20 to show your understanding of $\frac{3}{4}$ meter.

- Listen as each student reads his or her introduction to "My America." As a class, decide which introduction should be read at a performance.

My America

For 2-Part and Piano

Arranged with new words by
JOYCE EILERS

Words by SAMUEL F. SMITH
Based on "America"

Pur-ple moun - tain maj - es - ties, am-ber waves of grain.

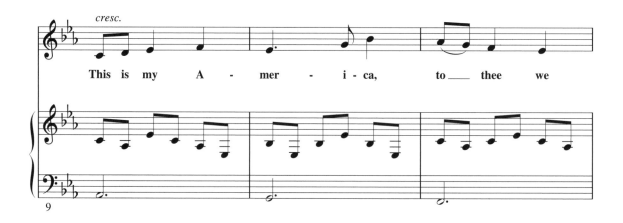

This is my A - mer - i - ca, to —— thee we

Pur-ple moun - tain maj - es - ties, am-ber waves of grain.

My coun - try 'tis of thee, sweet land of lib - er - ty,

This is my A - mer - i - ca, of ____ thee I

of thee I sing.

sing. Land ____ of the free from

Land where my fa - thers died,

land   be bright   with ___ free - dom's   ho - ly light,

land   be bright   with free - dom's   ho - ly light,

52

pro - tect us   by   Thy might,   great God our

pro - tect __ us __   by   Thy might,   great __ God our

55

rit.   *f*   *no decresc.*

King.   My A - mer - i - ca!

rit.   *f*   *no decresc.*

King.   My A - mer - i - ca!

rit.   *f*   *no decresc.*

58

Arranging

In music, an **arrangement** is *a composition in which a composer takes an existing melody and adds extra features or changes the melody in some way.* Composer Joyce Eilers wrote an arrangement of the familiar tune "My Country 'tis of Thee" by using the following techniques:

- Adding a piano accompaniment that supports the melody line.

- Writing a **descant** (*a special part that is usually sung higher than the melody*).

- Changing the key of the piece the second time the melody is sung.

- Writing a special ending sometimes referred to as a coda.

Study the music to "My America" found on pages 14–19. Identify the features mentioned above.

Other techniques that a composer may use in writing an arrangement of an existing melody is to lower or raise the pitch to make it easier to sing. A composer may take a vocal song and add instruments, or rearrange the song for instruments only. Sometimes a composer will change the time signature or meter, which may result in an arrangement that sounds quite different from the original.

In the example below, the familiar tune "My Country 'tis of Thee" has been changed from $\frac{3}{4}$ meter to $\frac{4}{4}$ meter, thus creating a new arrangement. Sing the example.

My coun-try 'tis of thee, sweet land of li - ber-ty of thee I sing.

On your own, complete this arrangement of "My Country 'tis of Thee" in $\frac{4}{4}$ meter. Think of another familiar melody and write an arrangement using some of the techniques suggested on this page.

SPOTLIGHT

Breath Management

Vocal sound is produced by air flowing between the vocal cords; therefore, correct breathing is important for good singing. Good breath management provides you with the support needed to sing expressively and for longer periods of time.

To experience, explore and establish proper breathing for singing, try the following:

- Put your hands on your waist at the bottom of your rib cage.

- Take in an easy breath for four counts, as if through a straw, without lifting your chest or shoulders.

- Feel your waist and rib cage expand all the way around like an inflating inner tube.

- Let your breath out slowly on "sss," feeling your "inner tube" deflating as if it has a slow leak.

- Remember to keep your chest up the entire time.

- Take in another easy breath for four counts before your "inner tube" has completely deflated, then let your air out on "sss" for eight counts.

- Repeat this step several times, taking in an easy breath for four counts and gradually increasing the number of counts to let your air out to sixteen counts.

Sometimes in singing it is necessary to take a quick or "catch" breath.

- Look out the window and imagine seeing something wonderful for the first time, like snow.

- Point your finger at the imaginary something and let in a quick, silent breath that expresses your wonderment and surprise.

- A quick breath is not a gasping breath, but rather a silent breath.

Music Alone Shall Live

Composer: Shirley W. McRae
Text: Traditional
Voicing: Unison Voices/3-Part Canon

VOCABULARY

unison

canon

a cappella

scale

trio

 SKILL BUILDERS

To learn more about the key of C major, see Beginning Sight-Singing, *pages 4 and 14.*

Focus

• Identify and perform a canon.

• Read and write music notation.

Getting Started

In a choir, there are many ways to sing. You can sing in **unison,** which means *all parts sing the same notes at the same time.* Or, you can sing a canon. A **canon** is *a form of music in which one part sings a melody and the other parts sing the same melody, but enter at different times.* Canons are sometimes called rounds. Singing in a canon is sometimes difficult because it is easy to lose track of your own part and join the others. However, when each singer can successfully stay on his or her own part, beautiful music is created.

◆ History and Culture

While "Music Alone Shall Live" can be sung with piano accompaniment, it can also be sung **a cappella**, or *without accompaniment.* This style of singing dates back hundreds of years, to when music was sung a cappella in the early European churches. In fact, this is where the term originated. In Latin, the word *a cappella* means "of the chapel." Today, a cappella singing encompasses a wide variety of musical styles, including barbershop, vocal jazz, gospel and others.

Links to Learning

◆ ## Vocal

Read and perform the melodic patterns below. Which pattern is found at the beginning of "Music Alone Shall Live?"

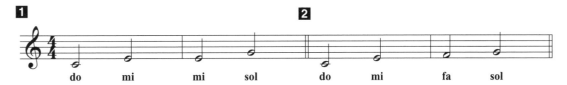

do mi mi sol   do mi fa sol

◆ ## Theory

This song is in the key of C major and is based on the C major scale. A **scale** is *a group of notes that are sung in succession and are based on a particular home tone*. The C major scale is easy to play on a piano or keyboard because this scale uses all white keys. To locate "C" on a piano, find any set of two black keys. "C" is the white key just to the left. Using the keyboard below as a guide, play the C major scale.

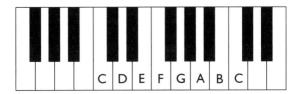

Sing the C major scale.

C D E F G A B C B A G F E D C
do re mi fa sol la ti do ti la sol fa mi re do

Evaluation

Demonstrate how well you have learned the skills and concepts featured in the lesson "Music Alone Shall Live" by completing the following:

• In your own words, describe a canon.

• Form a **trio**, or *a group of three singers*. Sing "Music Alone Shall Live" to show that you are able to stay on your own part.

• Based on the key of C major, write the pitches *do-mi-fa-sol* on a music staff.

Music Alone Shall Live

For Unison Voices/3-Part Canon and Piano

Traditional

Music by SHIRLEY W. McRAE

mu - sic ___ a - lone shall live. Mu - sic, mu - sic,

mu - sic a - lone shall live.

29 Canon in 3 parts *

Part I

Mu - sic, mu - sic, mu - sic a - lone shall live.

Part II

Part III

29

*May be performed with or without piano accompaniment.

Mu - sic, mu - sic, mu - sic a - lone shall live.

Mu - sic, mu - sic, mu - sic a - lone shall live.

33

Mu - sic, mu - sic, mu - sic a - lone shall live.

Mu - sic, mu - sic, mu - sic a - lone shall live.

Mu - sic, mu - sic, mu - sic a - lone shall live.

37

Mu - sic, mu - sic, mu - sic a - lone shall live.

Mu - sic, mu - sic, mu - sic a - lone shall live.

Mu - sic, mu - sic, mu - sic a - lone shall live.

last time rit.　　　　　　　　　*(repeat ad lib.)*

Mu - sic, mu - sic, mu - sic a - lone shall live.

last time rit.

Mu - sic, mu - sic, mu - sic a - lone shall live.

last time rit.

Mu - sic, mu - sic, mu - sic a - lone shall live.

(repeat ad lib.)

last time rit.

Singabahambayo

Composer: South African Folk Song
Text: Traditional Nguni
Voicing: Unison Voices with Optional 2-Part/3-Part

VOCABULARY
interval
syncopation

Focus

• Relate music to society.

• Read and perform syncopation.

• Perform music representing South African culture.

 **SKILL BUILDERS**

To learn more about syncopation, see Beginning Sight-Singing, *page 132.*

Getting Started

This is an imaginary story that takes place not so long ago. It is a story about a young person of color named Mary who is a native inhabitant of the country of South Africa. She lives with her mother in a rural area, but her father must live and work in the city. When Mary and her family go into the city, her mother must have a special pass to go shopping or to visit Mary's father. As a woman, Mary's mother is not allowed to work in the city, to vote, or to socialize with anyone outside her race.

Then, the situation changes in South Africa, and Mary and her family are offered a lifestyle of equality and freedom. In what ways might Mary express this new freedom? She could sing "Singabahambayo," which is a song of celebration—a celebration of freedom.

◆ History and Culture

For many decades, South Africa was a place of social and political turmoil. This struggle affected men, women and children. As outsiders moved into the area, apartheid, or the separation of people by race, developed. Soon the native inhabitants were deprived of their land, their jobs and their rights. Men were used as inexpensive labor to work in the gold and diamond mines. Finally, after much struggle and violent protest, all South Africans gained freedom and equal rights on April 27, 2001.

Links to Learning

◆ Vocal

An **interval** is *the distance between two notes*. Read and perform the following melodic patterns to practice singing intervals in tune.

do   re   mi   do   do   re   ti   do   mi   do

◆ Theory

Read and perform the following example to practice rhythmic patterns that contain syncopation. **Syncopation** is *the placement of accents on a weak beat or a weak portion of the beat.*

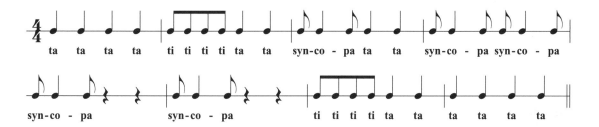

ta   ta   ta   ta   ti ti ti ti ta   ta   syn-co - pa   ta   ta   syn-co - pa syn-co - pa

syn-co - pa   syn-co - pa   ti ti ti ti ta   ta   ta   ta   ta   ta

◆ Artistic Expression

Movement can enhance the interpretation or character of a song. Form two or three circles in the room. Walk to the beat of a drum. Once you are secure in walking the beat, begin singing "Singabahambayo." Notice the words that occur on the first beat of each measure. Stress these words as you sing and walk.

Evaluation

Demonstrate how well you have learned the skills and concepts featured in the lesson "Singabahambayo" by completing the following:

- Individually perform the rhythmic patterns found in the Theory section above to test your ability to read syncopated rhythms.

- South African music is known for its strong sense of the beat and its overall rhythmic excitement. Apply what you have learned about this style of music by indicating the words or syllables that occur on the strong beats. Check your choices with your teacher. How accurate were you?

Singabahambayo

For Unison Voices with Optional 2-Part/3-Part and Piano

Piano arrangement by
MICHAEL SPRESSER

South African Folk Song
English words by JOHN HIGGINS

*Accompaniment CD has two measures fill before downbeat of measure 1.

*May be sung in unison or with optional harmony.

Diction

Singing is a form of communication. To communicate well while singing, you must not only form your vowels correctly, but also say your consonants as clearly and cleanly as possible.

There are two kinds of consonants: voiced and unvoiced. Consonants that require the use of the voice along with the **articulators** *(lips, teeth, tongue, and other parts of the mouth and throat)* are called voiced consonants. If you place your hand on your throat, you can actually feel your voice box vibrate while producing them. Unvoiced consonant sounds are made with the articulators only.

In each pair below, the first word contains a voiced consonant while the second word contains an unvoiced consonant. Speak the following word pairs, then sing them on any pitch. When singing, make sure the voiced consonant is on the same pitch as the vowel.

Voiced:	Unvoiced Consonants:	More Voiced Consonants:
[b] bay	[p] pay	[l] lip
[d] den	[t] ten	[m] mice
[g] goat	[k] coat	[n] nice
[dʒ] jeer	[tʃ] cheer	[j] yell
[z] zero	[s] scenic	[r] red
[ʒ] fusion	[ʃ] shun	
[ð] there	[θ] therapy	More Unvoiced Consonants:
[v] vine	[f] fine	[h] have
[w] wince	[hw] whim	

The American "r" requires special treatment in classical choral singing. To sing an American "r" at the end of a syllable following a vowel, sing the vowel with your teeth apart and jaw open. In some formal sacred music and English texts, you may need to flip or roll the "r." For most other instances, sing the "r" on pitch, then open to the following vowel quickly.

Good Cheer

Composer: Late Medieval English Song, arranged by Audrey Snyder
Text: Audrey Snyder
Voicing: 2-Part, Any Combination

VOCABULARY

Medieval period

a cappella

lute

intonation

$\frac{6}{8}$ meter

MUSIC&HISTORY

To learn more about the Medieval and Renaissance periods, see
page 106.

Focus

- Describe and perform music from the Medieval period.
- Read, write and perform music in $\frac{6}{8}$ meter.
- Interpret musical content through drama.

Getting Started

Imagine you are living in 14th century England. His Lordship, the Duke of Gloucester, is having a banquet, and you have been invited! The parchment invitation, secured with the Duke's own sealing wax, was delivered yesterday by a steward. What will you wear? What will you bring? What will you say? What kind of music will be performed? No doubt you would sing and dance to a song similar to "Good Cheer."

◆ History and Culture

This joyful piece is based upon a song entitled "Edi Be Thu," which was written in Gloucestershire, England during the **Medieval period** *(400–1430)*. Vocal music of this period was sometimes performed **a cappella**, or *without instrumental accompaniment*. At other times, it would not have been uncommon for a wooden flute or a **lute**, *an early form of the guitar*, to double the vocal parts. A drum would have been used to maintain the steady beat. When you perform "Good Cheer," try singing it a cappella and then again with instrumental accompaniment. Discuss which way you like the best.

Links to Learning

◆ Vocal

"Good Cheer" is in the key of F major and is based on the F major scale. To locate "F" on a piano, find any set of three black keys. "F" is the white key just to the left. This scale uses the notes F, G, A, B♭, C, D, E, F. Using the keyboard below as a guide, play the F major scale.

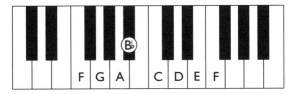

Sing the following scale, paying attention to **intonation,** or *in-tune singing.*

F	G	A	B♭	C	D	E	F	E	D	C	B♭	A	G	F
do	re	mi	fa	sol	la	ti	do	ti	la	sol	fa	mi	re	do

◆ Theory

Read and perform the following rhythmic pattern to practice reading music in **6/8 meter,** *a time signature in which there are six beats per measure and the dotted quarter note receives the beat.*

tam	tam	ti	ti	ti	tam	ta	ti	ti	ti	ti	tik-um	ti	tam

Evaluation

Demonstrate how well you have learned the skills and concepts featured in the lesson "Good Cheer" by completing the following:

- Discuss the musical characteristics of the Medieval period.

- Write four measures of rhythmic patterns in 6/8 meter. Use the music as a guide. Perform your composition for the class.

- With four to six friends, create a short skit about life in medieval Gloucester that ends with singing the first verse of "Good Cheer." Your characters might include the Duke, a weaver, a goldsmith, a blacksmith or a friar.

Good Cheer
(Festival Procession)

For 2-Part, Any Combination, with Piano* and Optional Hand Percussion**

Arranged by
AUDREY SNYDER

Words by AUDREY SNYDER
Based on a Late Medieval English Song

*May be sung a cappella.
**Hand Percussion parts found on page 41.

all___ good cheer!
in___ this hall.

all___ good cheer!
in___ this hall.

Good Cheer
(Festival Procession)

HAND PERCUSSION
(Hand Drum, Finger Cymbals)

Words by AUDREY SNYDER
Based on a Late Medieval English Song
Arranged by AUDREY SYNDER

Winter's Night

Composer: Frode Fjellheim
Text: Frode Fjellheim
Voicing: 2-Part

VOCABULARY

yoik

diction

perfect fifth

Focus

- Relate music to culture.

- Sing with good diction.

- Perform music from the Arctic region of Sampi.

 SKILL BUILDERS

To learn more about the key of D minor, see Beginning Sight-Singing, page 50.

Getting Started

In the month of December, how many hours of daylight does your location receive? What time is light visible? What time does darkness return? Imagine living in the Arctic Circle, where for two months during the winter, the sun barely rises above the horizon, leaving the daytime in darkness. Winter begins in October and extends through May. Temperatures may get as cold as 60° F *below* zero. Lakes and rivers are frozen, and the snow that covers the landscape mutes sound. According to the composer, "Winter's Night" musically paints a picture of the silence and darkness during such a winter.

◆ History and Culture

"Winter's Night" loosely models the style of a **yoik**, *a vocal tradition of the Sami people.* The Sami are some of the original inhabitants of the Arctic region called Sampi (formerly referred to as Lapland), which includes the northernmost sections of Norway, Sweden and Finland, as well as Russia's Kola Peninsula. The yoik vocal tradition typically features short melodic phrases that are repeated with slight variations. The text of "Winter's Night" uses syllables that have no meaning, but are designed to sound like the Norwegian language.

Links to Learning

◆ Vocal

In vocal music, **diction** is *the pronunciation of words while singing.* Read and perform the following examples to practice singing with good diction.

1

no	vai - ja	vai - ja	na	vai - ja	na	na	vai - ja	na
noo	*vah_ee-yah*	*vah_ee-yah*	*nah*	*vah_ee-yah*	*nah*	*nah*	*vah_ee-yah*	*nah*

2

no	vai - la	vai - la	na	vai - la	na	na	vai - la	na
noo	*vah_ee-lah*	*vah_ee-lah*	*nah*	*vah_ee-lah*	*nah*	*nah*	*vah_ee-lah*	*nah*

3

no	vai - a	vai - a	na	vai - a	na	na	vai - a	na
noo	*vah_ee-ah*	*vah_ee-ah*	*nah*	*vah_ee-ah*	*nah*	*nah*	*vah_ee-ah*	*nah*

4

ha	na	nai - ja	nai - ja	nai - ja	ha	na	nai - ja	na
hah	*nah*	*nah_ee-yah*	*nah_ee-yah*	*nah_ee-yah*	*hah*	*nah*	*nah_ee-yah*	*nah*

◆ Theory

"Winter's Night" is in the key of D minor and is based on the D minor scale. Read and perform the first example to establish the key of D minor. **A perfect fifth** is *the interval of two pitches that are five notes apart on the staff.* Read and perform the second example to practice singing perfect fifths in tune.

1

D	E	F	G	A	B♭	C	D	C	B♭	A	G	F	E	D
la	ti	do	re	mi	fa	sol	la	sol	fa	mi	re	do	ti	la

2

mi re do ti la	la ti do re mi	la	do	mi	do	la	mi	la

Evaluation

Demonstrate how well you have learned the skills and concepts featured in the lesson "Winter's Night" by completing the following:

- Discuss ways in which the music paints a picture of the silence and darkness of the long, harsh winters of Sampi.

- Perform your part in measures 48–64 to show you can sing with good diction.

From NORWEGIAN SAMI SONGS

Winter's Night
(Vinternatt)

For 2-Part and Piano with Optional B♭ Soprano Saxophone and Triangle*

**Words and Music by
FRODE FJELLHEIM**

* Instrument parts found on pages 53–55.

Vai-ja na   na vai-ja na   vai-ja na ja no

vai-ja na - ja vai-ja na   vai-ja na   ja no   Vai-ja na   na

vai-ja na - ja   vai-ja na   vai-ja na   ja   no _____

_____   ha   na _____

vai-ja na_____ ja no_____

ja - a no_____

From NORWEGIAN SAMI SONGS

Winter's Night
(Vinternatt)

Bb Soprano Saxophone (Bb Clarinet)

Music by
FRODE FJELLHEIM

From NORWEGIAN SAMI SONGS

Winter's Night

(Vinternatt)

Instrumental Part in C

Music by
FRODE FJELLHEIM

54 Beginning Unison, 2-Part/3-Part

From NORWEGIAN SAMI SONGS
Winter's Night
(Vinternatt)

Triangle

Music by
FRODE FJELLHEIM

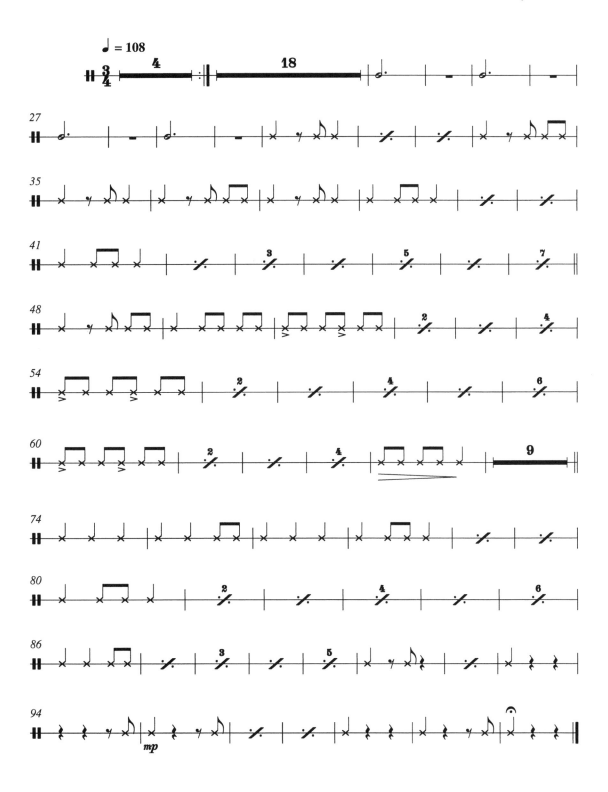

Radiator Lions

Composer: Michael Jothen (b. 1944)
Text: Dorothy Aldis
Voicing: Unison Voices

VOCABULARY

Contemporary
   period

rondo form

music notation

Focus

- Describe and perform music from the Contemporary period.
- Identify rondo form.
- Use nontraditional notation to read, write and perform music.

*To learn more about the
Contemporary period,
see page 122.*

Getting Started

Some common ways to express yourself with your voice are whispering, speaking, singing, and shouting. But if you imitate the sound of an airplane, a school bell or a siren, you use your voice in a different way. Try making these sounds with your voice.

The word *traditional* describes characteristics common to a specific time or concept, whereas *nontraditional* describes characteristics that are uncommon. For example, two houses may have the same number of rooms, but may look different due to the style used to create them. In the traditional house, you might find walls, a roof and windows, while the nontraditional house might be built into the side of a hill or underground.

◆ History and Culture

"Radiator Lions" is a musical composition from the **Contemporary period** *(1900–present)*. A common practice in this period is to combine traditional and nontraditional elements in the same piece of music. This song is written in a traditional form known as rondo form. **Rondo form** is *a musical form in which a repeated section is separated by several contrasting sections.* If you were to divide this song into sections, it might look something like this: A, B, A, C, A. Through the use of nontraditional **music notation**, or *a means of writing down music*, you will see how to produce a variety of sounds with your voice. Find examples of this notation in the music.

Links to Learning

◆ Theory

Read and perform the following example to develop rhythmic precision.

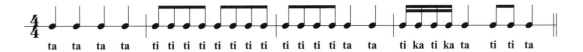

ta ta ta ta ti ti ti ti ti ti ti ti ti ti ti ti ta ta ti ka ti ka ta ti ti ta

◆ Artistic Expression

Study the following definitions to help you interpret nontraditional music notation.

1 ♩ = Speak

2 ⌒ = Get louder and softer according to the rise and fall of the line

3 ∿∿∿ = Continue making the sound until instructed to stop

4 = Speak with inflection

Read and perform the following example to practice speaking with inflection. Make your voice sound higher and lower based on the rise and fall of the notes.

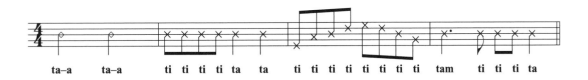

ta–a ta–a ti ti ti ti ta ta ti ti ti ti ti ti ti ti tam ti ti ti ta

Evaluation

Demonstrate how well you have learned the skills and concepts featured in the lesson "Radiator Lions" by completing the following:

- Discuss the musical characteristics of the Contemporary period.

- Look in the music to find sections that are repeated and sections that are different. Label the sections that make up the rondo form in this piece.

- On a piece of staff paper, create nontraditional music notation for the sounds of an airplane, a school bell and a siren. Share your notation with other members of the class.

Radiator Lions

For Unison Voices and Piano

Words by DOROTHY ALDIS

Music by MICHAEL JOTHEN

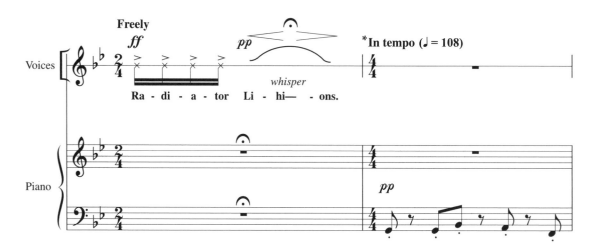

* CD accompaniment starts here.

*Forearm thrusts on black notes on keyboard; actual note ranges are approximate.

† Pause CD track at this point.

* Divide choir into two parts. Group II should double the size of Group I. Members of Group II should perform as many of the sounds, as many times as possible, before being stopped. These should be as loud as possible.

† Start CD here to continue.

SPOTLIGHT

Vocal Production

There are many ways we can use our voices to communicate. We can speak, shout, laugh, whisper, sigh and sing. This lesson will focus on your singing voice. It is best to think of singing as extended speech so you do not put too much physical effort into it.

Perform the following exercises to experience, explore and establish singing as extended speech.

- Say the phrase "Hello, my name is _____" as if you were greeting someone enthusiastically.

- Say the phrase again, but speak all of it on the same pitch as the first syllable.

- Repeat the phrase, making sure you take a singer's breath before you start.

- Feel the flow of the breath as it smoothly connects each word to the next.

- Try the phrase several times, starting on different pitches, seeing how long you can hold out your name.

- Remember to keep your chest high and your "inner tube" inflated for as long as you can. (It will feel like a belt is tightening around your waist the longer you hold it.)

Explore your **head voice** (*the singer's higher singing voice*) and your **chest voice** (*the singer's lower singing voice*) by performing the following exercises.

- Place your upper teeth on your lower lip as if you were going to say the letter "v."

- Make a singing tone on a lower pitch for a few seconds, keeping your teeth on your lower lip.

- Now, take a singer's breath and start the "v" sound on a lower pitch, but immediately move the pitch upward as high as you can go.

- Repeat the last step, this time bringing the voice back down low again.

- Notice the stretching feeling you have in your throat as you go higher and lower.

Jesu, Joy of Man's Desiring

Composer: Johann Sebastian Bach (1685–1750), arranged by Henry Leck
Text: Verse 6 of *Jesu, meiner Seelen Wonne* by Martin Jahn (1661)
Voicing: Unison Voices/2-Part

VOCABULARY

cantata

Baroque period

legato

triplet

phrase

To learn more about the Baroque period, see page 110.

Focus

• Describe and perform music from the Baroque period.

• Read and write triplets.

• Sing phrases expressively.

Getting Started

What do the following activities have in common?

• Taking out the garbage
• Going to a piano lesson
• Reading the Sunday comics

If you guessed "things you do once a week," you're right. What other activities would you personally add to the list?

◆ History and Culture

If you were Johann Sebastian Bach (1685–1750), you could include "composing a cantata" on your list. Now this may not seem too difficult for one of the world's greatest composers, but a **cantata** is *a musical piece made up of several movements for singers and instrumentalists* that can last over 20 minutes. While working as a church musician in Germany, Bach's job included writing a cantata for every church service. He also wrote cantatas for other special occasions. Over 200 of his cantatas are still in publication. "Jesu, Joy of Man's Desiring" is a part of Bach's *Cantata 147*.

Bach lived during the **Baroque period** *(1600–1750)*. Music of the Baroque period frequently features a simple melody, supported by a fancy accompaniment with a continuously moving bass line. Many large works, including cantatas, were developed during this period.

Links to Learning

◆ Vocal

Perform the following example to practice singing in a **legato** (*connected and sustained*) style.

noo   noo   noo   noo   noo   noo   noo   noo

◆ Theory

Perform the following examples to practice rhythmic patterns found in "Jesu, Joy of Man's Desiring," which include **triplets** (*three eighth notes per beat*). Form two groups. At the same time, one group taps the steady beat while the other group claps the rhythms. Switch roles.

◆ Artistic Expression

A **phrase** is *a musical idea with a beginning and an end*. Sing the phrase in measures 9–12 of "Jesu, Joy of Man's Desiring" while drawing an arch in the air above your head. Shape your phrase by beginning softly at measure 9. Your phrase should be loudest at the highest point of your arch and softest at its lowest point.

Evaluation

Demonstrate how well you have learned the skills and concepts featured in the lesson "Jesu, Joy of Man's Desiring" by completing the following:

• Discuss the musical characteristics of the Baroque period.

• Write a four-measure rhythmic phrase in $\frac{3}{4}$ meter that includes two to four triplets. Perform your phrase for others in the class.

• Find other phrases in the music. Select one person to come forward and serve as a "phrase leader." Sing each phrase while following the arch shown by the phrase leader. How expressively were you able to sing the phrases?

As Recorded by THE CANADIAN BRASS and THE INDIANAPOLIS CHILDREN'S CHOIR
Henry Leck, Conductor

Jesu, Joy Of Man's Desiring

from *CANTATA 147*

For Unison/2-Part and Piano

Arranged by HENRY LECK
Piano Arrangement by DEAN CROCKER

JOHANN SEBASTIAN BACH (1685–1750)
Brass Accompaniment by FREDERICK MILLS

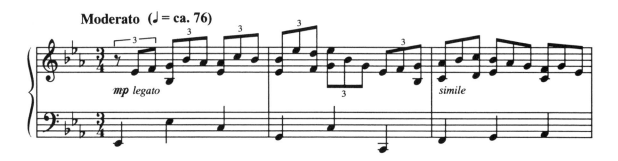

life___ im - pas - sion'd.
ho___ liest trea - sure.

life___ im - pas - sion'd.
ho___ liest trea - sure.

52

Striv - ing still to Truth___ un - known,
Thou dost e - ver lead___ Thine own,

Striv - ing still to Truth___ un - known,
Thou dost e - ver lead___ Thine own,

dim.

soar - ing, dy - ing round___ Thy
in the love___ of joys___ un -

dim.

soar - ing, dy - ing round Thy___
in the love___ of joys un -

dim.

60

throne.
known.

throne.
known.

opt. repeat

opt. repeat

Da pacem Domine

Composer: Melchior Franck (c. 1579–1639), arranged by Emily Crocker
Text: Traditional Latin
Voicing: For 2, 3 or 4-Part, Any Combination

VOCABULARY

harmony

canon

Baroque period

stepwise motion

skipwise motion

Focus

- Identify and perform a canon.
- Explain and demonstrate stepwise and skipwise motion.

 SPOTLIGHT

To learn more about careers in music, see page 175.

Getting Started

There are many ways to sing in harmony. **Harmony** is *a musical sound that is formed when two or more different pitches are sung at the same time.* A canon, sometimes known as a round, is a great way to sing in harmony. In a **canon,** *one part sings a melody. Then, another part sings the same melody, entering a short time after the first part has begun.*

"Da pacem Domine" is an excellent example of a canon. Written in Latin, it was composed almost 500 years ago. Translated, the text means, "Give us peace, O Lord, in our days." How do these words still hold meaning for us today?

◆ History and Culture

Melchior Franck (c. 1579–1639) was a well-known German composer who lived during the early **Baroque period** *(1600–1750).* He wrote over 600 pieces of choral music. Franck served at the court of Coburg as Kapellmeister (master of the chapel or director of music) for the majority of his life.

Latin is sometimes used in choral music because of its pure vowel sounds. Vowels are the foundation of a good choral tone. Singing vowels properly will help you blend well with others in your choir to create a pleasing sound.

Links to Learning

◆ Vocal

Perform the following example to practice singing vowels in Latin.

Da pa - cem Do - mi - ne,   da pa - cem Do - mi - ne in di - e - bus   no - stris.
dah pah-chem daw-mee-neh,   dah pah-chem daw-mee-neh een dee - eh - boos   naw - strees

◆ Theory

Stepwise motion is *the movement from a given note to the next note above or below it on the staff.* Look at the example below. Notice that the notes move from a space to the next line or from a line to the next space. Read and perform the following example to practice singing in stepwise motion.

do   re   mi   fa   sol   fa   mi   re   do

Skipwise motion is *the movement from a given note to another note that is two or more notes above or below it on the staff.* Look at the example below. Notice that most of the notes do not move from a space to the next line or from a line to the next space. Read and perform the following example to practice singing in skipwise motion.

do   mi   sol   mi   sol   fa   re   mi   do   re   do

Evaluation

Demonstrate how well you have learned the skills and concepts featured in the lesson "Da pacem Domine" by completing the following:

- Select a canon that you already know. With a group of your friends, perform the canon for the class.

- Locate in "Da pacem Domine" examples of stepwise and skipwise motion. Sing one example of each.

Da pacem Domine

For 2, 3 or 4-Part, Any Combination, a cappella

Arranged by EMILY CROCKER

MELCHIOR FRANCK (c. 1579–1639)

*To perform as a 4-part canon, each part may enter in the order shown.

Vowels

The style of a given piece of music dictates how we should pronounce the words. If we are singing a more formal, classical piece, then we need to form taller vowels as in very proper English. If we are singing in a jazz or pop style, then we should pronounce the words in a more relaxed, conversational way. To get the feeling of taller vowels for classical singing, do the following:

- Let your jaw gently drop down and back as if it were on a hinge.

- Place your hands on your cheeks beside the corners of your mouth.

- Sigh on an *ah* [ɑ] vowel sound, but do not spread the corners of your mouth.

- Now sigh on other vowel sounds—*eh* [ɛ], *ee* [i], *oh* [o] and *oo* [u]—keeping the back of the tongue relaxed.

- As your voice goes from higher notes to lower notes, think of gently opening a tiny umbrella inside your mouth.

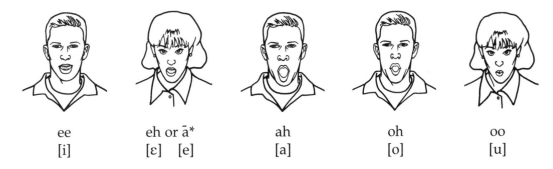

ee	eh or ā*	ah	oh	oo
[i]	[ɛ] [e]	[ɑ]	[o]	[u]

Other vowel sounds used in singing are diphthongs. A **diphthong** is *a combination of two vowel sounds.* For example, the vowel *ay* consists of two sounds: *eh* [E] and *ee* [i]. To sing a diphthong correctly, stay on the first vowel sound for the entire length of the note, only lightly adding the second vowel sound as you move to another note or lift off the note.

I = *ah*_____(ee) [ɑi]

boy = *oh*_____(ee) [oi]

down = *ah*_____(oo) [ɑu]

*Note: This is an Italian "ā," which is one sound, and not an American "ā," which is a diphthong, or two sounds.

Sanctus

Composer: Franz Schubert (1797–1828), arranged by Donald Moore
Text: Traditional Latin
Voicing: 2-Part

VOCABULARY

Romantic period

mass

sequence

melodic contour

duet

MUSIC&**HISTORY**

To learn more about the Romantic period, see page 118.

Focus

• Describe and perform music from the Romantic period.

• Identify and demonstrate melodic contour.

• Sing independently in duets.

Getting Started

If you like…	*You could thank …*
To ride your bicycle	Baron Karl von Drais
To work with computers	Mr. Alan Turing
To eat chocolate	Mr. Milton Hershey

And if you like to sing, you could thank Mr. Franz Schubert!

◆ History and Culture

Born in Vienna, Austria, Franz Schubert (1797–1828) can be considered one of the best songwriters of all time. Schubert wrote over 600 songs with harmonies and rhythms that perfectly capture the mood and meaning of the words. His music is also filled with spinning, lyrical melodies. With its expressiveness, complex harmonies and rich sound, Schubert's music is an important part of the early **Romantic period** *(1820–1900)*.

The Sanctus is the text from one section of the **mass**, *a religious service of prayers and ceremonies*. A common language of the mass is Latin. Although Latin is not a modern spoken language, its pure vowels make it a favorite of singers. Composers throughout the centuries have set the words of the Sanctus to music. So, if you find yourself singing the beautiful melody of this "Sanctus," don't forget to thank Franz Schubert!

Links to Learning

◆ Vocal

Read and perform the following examples to practice singing two of the melodic patterns found in "Sanctus." Find these patterns in the music.

do   sol   mi   do   sol   mi   do re mi

◆ Theory

A **sequence** is *a successive musical pattern that begins on a higher or lower pitch each time it is repeated.* Perform the following example to practice singing a sequence. Find the sequences in "Sanctus."

loo loo loo loo loo   loo loo   loo loo loo loo loo   loo loo   loo loo loo loo loo   loo   loo   loo

◆ Artistic Expression

Be choir directors! While your teacher sings measures 7–12, show the **melodic contour**, or *the overall shape of the melody*, by using conducting motions. Then, as a choir, continue to conduct while you sing this passage, expressing the melodic contour of the piece through your voices.

Evaluation

Demonstrate how well you have learned the skills and concepts featured in the lesson "Sanctus" by completing the following:

- Discuss the musical characteristics of the Romantic period.

- Create a dance or movement performance that shows the melodic contour of "Sanctus."

- Expressively sing "Sanctus" as a **duet** (*two singers with one singer on each of two parts*).

Sanctus

For 2-Part and Piano and Optional Flute or C Instrument*

**Arranged with additional music
by DONALD MOORE**

Traditional Latin
Based on a canon by FRANZ SCHUBERT (1797–1828)

*Flute part found on page 82.

Sanctus

FLUTE (C INSTRUMENT)

Traditional Latin
Based on a canon by FRANZ SCHUBERT (1797– 1828)
Arranged with additional music by DONALD MOORE

SPOTLIGHT

Pitch Matching

As you begin to learn how to read music, you must learn not only how to identify the notes on the printed page, but also how to sing the notes you read in tune. Accurate pitch matching requires that you hear the note in your head before you sing it instead of trying to find the note with your voice. Learning to sing from one note to another in scale patterns will help you hear the notes in your head before you sing them. Perform the scale below first using note names, then numbers, and finally solfège syllables.

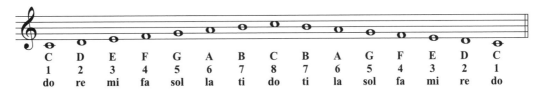

To help you sing the following examples on the correct pitch, hear the notes in your head before you sing them. If you cannot hear the interval skip in your head before you sing it, mentally sing the first note followed by all the notes in between until you come to the right note. Then, begin again and sing the pattern as written.

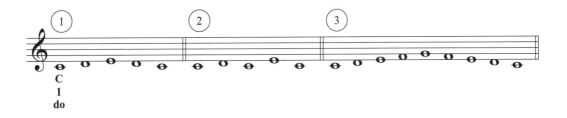

Alleluia

Composer: Wolfgang Amadeus Mozart (1756–1791), arranged by Henry Leck
Text: Traditional Latin
Voicing: 2-Part

VOCABULARY

Classical period

melisma

Focus

- Describe and perform music from the Classical period.
- Sing melismas correctly.
- Identify, read and perform sixteenth notes.

Getting Started

Imagine singing a song that uses only one word. How interesting do you think that would be? In "Alleluia," Wolfgang Amadeus Mozart—using only one word—created a masterpiece.

Many qualities of the **Classical period** *(1750–1820)* are found in the music of Mozart. One of these qualities is music that is light in character. Sometimes, this music contains melismas. A **melisma** is *many notes that are sung on one syllable or word.* Often, these fast-moving passages make this music challenging to sing. The use of melismas in the Classical period is shown in Mozart's "Alleluia."

MUSIC & HISTORY

To learn more about the Classical period, see page 114.

◆ History and Culture

Wolfgang Amadeus Mozart (1756–1791) is one of the most famous composers in Western music. He lived in Vienna, Austria, and worked as a professional musician during the late 1700s. He began composing music at the age of five. Mozart also wrote a wide variety of music for instruments and singers.

"Alleluia" is from Mozart's larger work, *Exsultate, jubilate.* He wrote this piece when he was just sixteen years old. Written in 1773, "Alleluia" is one of Mozart's most well-known pieces of vocal music.

Links to Learning

◆ Vocal

Read and perform the D major scale below to practice singing melismas. Begin slowly, then increase the speed as you are able.

1. tah   tah tah tah tah tah tah   tah   tah tah tah tah tah tah   tah
2. pah_____ pah_____   pah_____ pah_____   pah
3. lah_____   lah_____   lah

This arrangement of "Alleluia" is in the key of D major and is based on the D major scale. To locate "D" on the piano, find any set of two black keys. "D" is the white key between these two keys. This scale uses the notes D, E, F♯, G, A, B, C♯, D. Using the keyboard below as a guide, play the D major scale.

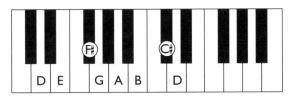

◆ Theory

Read and perform the following example to practice rhythmic patterns with sixteenth notes.

ti ka ti ka ti ka ti ka   ti   ti ka ti   ti   ti ka ti   ti ka ti   ti   ti ka ti   ti

ti ka ti   ti ka ti   ti   ti ka ti   ti   ti ka ti   ti ka ti ka   ta–a

Evaluation

Demonstrate how well you have learned the skills and concepts featured in the lesson "Alleluia" by completing the following:

- Discuss the musical characteristics of the Classical period.

- Sing the D major scale ascending and descending on "ah" to show that you can sing melismas with a light tone.

- Find the page in the music that contains the most sixteenth notes. Perform two measures to show that you can read rhythmic patterns with sixteenth notes.

From EXSULTATE, JUBILATE

Alleluia

For 2-Part and Piano

Arranged by
HENRY LECK

WOLFGANG AMADEUS MOZART
(1756–1791)

SPOTLIGHT

Melismas

Sing the first phrase of "My Country 'tis of Thee" as shown below. Notice that every syllable of the text receives exactly one note.

My coun-try 'tis of thee, sweet land of li - ber-ty of thee I sing.

This style of text setting is known as **syllabic** (*one syllable for every note*). Can you think of other songs with syllabic text settings?

When one syllable is given many pitches, this is referred to as melismatic singing. A **melisma** is *a group of notes sung to a single syllable*. Melismatic singing became popular in the Middle Ages (c. 400–1450), when as many as several dozen notes would have been sung on the final syllable of a Gregorian chant. The example below shows a melisma on the word "alleluia" similar to those found in Mozart's "Alleluia" on page 87.

Al - le - lu - ia.

When learning to sing a melisma, the key is to begin slowly. First, learn the pitches on syllables or numbers, and then, count-sing the rhythm of the melisma. Once your pitches and rhythms are secure, sing the melisma on a neutral syllable, such as "doo." Start at a slow tempo, gradually increasing your speed over several weeks. With each repetition, make sure every note is distinct, yet smoothly connected to one another. When you are able to sing the melisma clearly on "doo," switch to the syllable "ah." Once again, begin slowly, then gradually increase your speed to the performance tempo.

Singing a melisma is a vocal skill that may take time to master. With diligent practice, you will soon sing them musically and beautifully!

Waters Ripple and Flow

Composer: Slovakian Folk Song, arranged by Ruth Boshkoff
Text: Traditional
Voicing: 2-Part

VOCABULARY
folk song
descant

Focus

- Read rhythmic patterns with triplets and sixteenth notes
- Compose rhythmic phrases
- Perform music from different cultures

 **SKILL BUILDERS**

To learn more about sixteenth notes and triplets, see Beginning Sight-Singing, *pages 58 and 143.*

Getting Started

Have you ever played the "Telephone Game"? One person whispers a phrase into another's ear, and then that person whispers it to the next, and so forth. The last person to hear the phrase states what he or she has heard. It is fun to see how the phrase changes as it passes from one person to another.

Folk songs develop in a similar way. Throughout history, people have created songs about their everyday lives. **Folk songs** are *songs that have been passed down by word of mouth from generation to generation.* Parents would teach a song to their children, and their children would teach it to their children. As you can imagine, some folk songs have stayed very much the same, while others, just like the whispered phrases in the "Telephone Game," have changed as they have been passed from person to person.

◆ History and Culture

"Waters Ripple and Flow" is a folk song that came from Slovakia, in central Europe. In an attempt to keep the traditions and customs of their country alive, the people of Slovakia have developed a rich tradition of folk art, music, and dance. The melody of this beautiful song flows like the river that will bring the lonesome singer's true love back home.

Links to Learning

◆ Theory

Read and perform the following examples to get a feel for how the division of the beat moves from quarter notes to eighth notes, triplets and sixteenth notes. Step the beat as you perform.

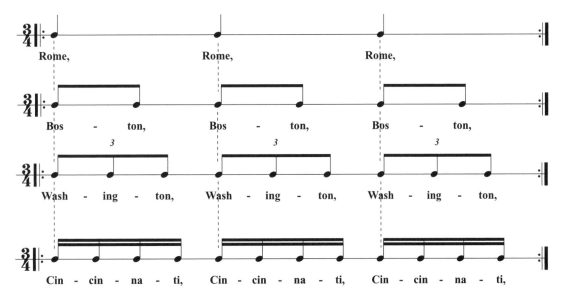

◆ Artistic Expression

To develop artistry through rhythmic chanting, organize into groups of four students. Within your group, select two different rhythmic patterns from the Vocal section above. Have half of your group chant one city name, while the other half claps another. Through this exercise, you will be able to get a feel for the complex rhythms found in "Waters Ripple and Flow."

Evaluation

Demonstrate how well you have learned the skills and concepts featured in the lesson "Waters Ripple and Flow" by completing the following:

- To show that you can read the rhythms used in this song, clap the rhythm of the **descant** (*a special part that is often higher than the other parts*) in measures 29–40.

- Think of some animals or foods whose syllables can represent different notes. For example, "corn" (quarter notes), "green beans" (eighth notes), "cantaloupe" (triplets), and "watermelon" (sixteenth notes). Write and perform two of these rhythmic patterns using the Theory section above as a guide. How did you do?

For Deb Shearer

Waters Ripple and Flow

For 2-Part and Piano

Arranged by
RUTH BOSHKOFF

Slovakian Folk Song

sea.   free.

22

26

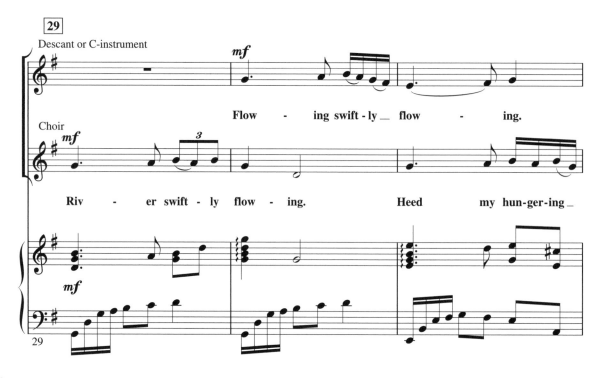

29

Descant or C-instrument

Flow - ing swift - ly _ flow - ing.

Choir

Riv - er swift - ly flow - ing.   Heed   my hun - ger - ing _

29

41

Solo or small group I

mf *3*

Wa - ters rip-ple and flow, so swift-ly they go, ____

Solo or small group II

mf *3*

Wa - ters rip-ple and flow so swift - ly, wa - ters rip-ple and

Choir *mp*

Ah, ____ ah, ____

41

mp

41

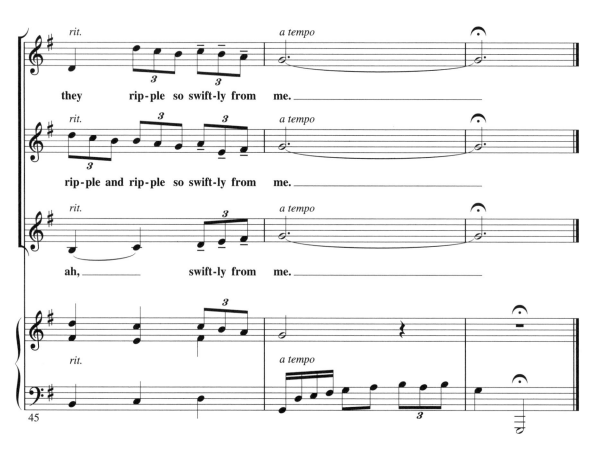

rit. *a tempo*

3 *3*

they rip-ple so swift-ly from me. ____

rit. *3* *3* *a tempo*

3

rip-ple and rip-ple so swift-ly from me. ____

rit. *3* *a tempo*

ah, ____ swift-ly from me. ____

3

rit. *a tempo*

3

45

Music & History

Links to Music

Leonardo da Vinci (1452–1519) was an Italian painter who lived in Florence and Milan during the Renaissance. In *Portrait of Cecilia Gallerani (Lady with an Ermine)*, da Vinci shows opposing motion as the upper body is turned to the viewer's left and the head faces the right. The small ermine is a symbol of purity and modesty. According to legend, ermines did not get dirty, and they ate only once a day. Notice the costume of the day, about 1490 A.D.

Leonardo da Vinci. *Portrait of Cecila Gallerani (Lady with an Ermine)*. c. 1490. Oil on wood. 54.8 x 40.3 cm (21 1/2 x 15 13/16"). Czartorychi Muzeum, Cracow, Poland.

RENAISSANCE c. 1430–1600

Focus
- Describe characteristics of Renaissance music.
- Relate music to history.

The Renaissance— A Time of Great Awakening

Can you imagine sailing across unexplored waters or creating a new invention? During the **Renaissance period** *(c. 1430–1600)*, the world experienced a time of rapid development in exploration, science, and the arts.

In 1425, Johann Gutenberg of Germany invented the printing press. Previously, to make a book, someone had to write it all by hand. It may have taken two months to produce one book. With the new printing press, books were mass-produced and became accessible to many people. The development of the compass made it possible for explorers to travel to new continents. In the early 1500s, Martin Luther led the Protestant Reformation, which caused important changes in religion, politics and music.

Among the famous people from the Renaissance who still influence our lives today are:

- Andrea Gabrieli—Italian composer
- Michelangelo and Leonardo da Vinci—Italian artists
- William Shakespeare—English playwright
- Nicolas Copernicus—Polish astronomer
- Ferdinand Magellan—Portuguese explorer

Looking Back— The Medieval Period

During the Medieval period (400–1430), also known as the Middle Ages, people in Western Europe thought of the Catholic church as the center of their lives. Much of the music written at this time was related to the church. One common form of music, the Gregorian chant, was a unison chant that was sung in Latin and performed **a cappella** *(with voices only; no accompaniment)*.

Outside the church, the music was often lively and sometimes accompanied by a drum, a wooden flute or a **lute** *(an early form of the guitar)*.

COMPOSERS
Josquin des Prez
(c. 1450–1521)

Andrea Gabrieli
(c. 1510–1586)

Michael Praetorius
(1571–1621)

Thomas Weelkes
(1575–1623)

ARTISTS
Gentile Bellini
(1429–1507)

Sandro Botticelli
(1445–1510)

Leonardo da Vinci
(1452–1519)

Michelangelo
(1475–1564)

Raphael
(1483–1520)

AUTHORS
Martin Luther
(1483–1546)

William Shakespeare
(1565–1616)

VOCABULARY
Renaissance period

a cappella

lute

sacred music

secular music

madrigal

polyphony

canzona

Renaissance Music

The music of the Renaissance falls into two categories: **sacred music**, or *music associated with religious services or themes*, and **secular music**, or *music not associated with religious services or themes*. Sacred music was very important during the Renaissance. Instruments such as organs, strings (lutes, viols, harps), and winds (recorders, sackbuts) began to accompany voices in church services. In Germany, Martin Luther introduced the use of the German language during the worship service, which had previously been exclusively in Latin. He also composed sacred songs in German so that the local people could sing and understand them.

Secular music also thrived during the Renaissance. A significant new type of music was the **madrigal**, *a poem that has been set to music in the language of the composer*. With the development of the madrigal, a new style of writing emerged. This style is known as **polyphony**, *a style of music in which there are two or more melodic lines being sung or played at the same time*. Each part begins at a different place and acts independently. This style of writing was very popular; as a result, the Renaissance period is often referred to as the "golden age of polyphony."

Performance Links

When performing music of the Renaissance period, it is important to apply the following guidelines:

- Sing with clarity and purity of tone.
- Balance the vocal lines with equal importance.
- In polyphonic music, sing the rhythms accurately and with precision.
- Perform a cappella, when written.

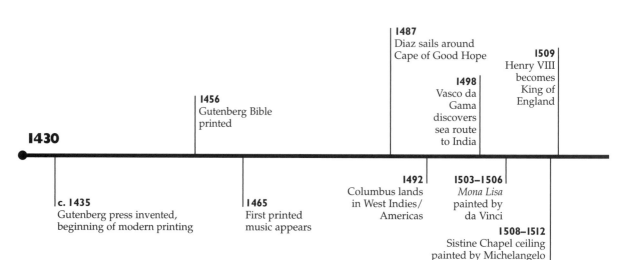

1487 Diaz sails around Cape of Good Hope

1509 Henry VIII becomes King of England

1498 Vasco da Gama discovers sea route to India

1456 Gutenberg Bible printed

1430

c. 1435 Gutenberg press invented, beginning of modern printing

1465 First printed music appears

1492 Columbus lands in West Indies/ Americas

1503–1506 *Mona Lisa* painted by da Vinci

1508–1512 Sistine Chapel ceiling painted by Michelangelo

Listening Links

CHORAL SELECTION

"El Grillo" by Josquin des Prez (c. 1450–1521)

Josquin des Prez was born in France, but worked in Italy, the Netherlands, and France as both a church and court musician. In his compositions, des Prez often used the music and text to imitate the sounds of nature. In "El Grillo," or "The Cricket," the music imitates the sound of crickets.

Published in 1504, "El Grillo" is an example of an early madrigal. It is performed a cappella. The text is in Italian, while the form is ABA. Can you hear the imitation of the crickets in this music? When does it occur?

INSTRUMENTAL SELECTION

"Canzon in Echo Duodecimi Toni a 10" by Giovanni Gabrieli (c. 1553–1612)

Giovanni Gabrieli was an important musician in Venice, Italy. He composed both sacred and secular music. Although much of his work is written for voice, he also wrote instrumental music. During the sixteenth century, the **canzona** (*a rhythmic instrumental composition that is light and fast-moving*) emerged. Canzonas are usually sectional in form and use imitation. The repetition of the opening section at the end is common. They are among the best of Gabrieli's music. Can you hear the repetition of the opening section at the end?

Check Your Understanding

1. Describe polyphony.

2. Analyze the Renaissance characteristics as heard in "El Grillo."

3. Compare the influence of the printing press during the Renaissance to the use of computers today.

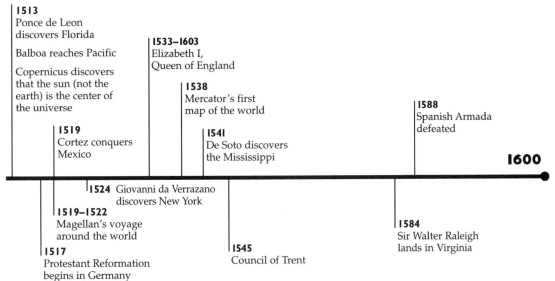

1513
Ponce de Leon
discovers Florida

Balboa reaches Pacific

Copernicus discovers
that the sun (not the
earth) is the center of
the universe

1519
Cortez conquers
Mexico

1533–1603
Elizabeth I,
Queen of England

1538
Mercator's first
map of the world

1541
De Soto discovers
the Mississippi

1588
Spanish Armada
defeated

1600

1524 Giovanni da Verrazano
discovers New York

1519–1522
Magellan's voyage
around the world

1517
Protestant Reformation
begins in Germany

1545
Council of Trent

1584
Sir Walter Raleigh
lands in Virginia

Jan Molenaer (c. 1610–1668) was a Dutch painter who was married to artist Judith Leyster (1609–1660). In this painting, the subject of children making music celebrates the carefree pleasures of youth. The boy on the left is playing a violin, while the one on the right plays a "rommelpot" (rumbling pot). The girl is playing an accompaniment by beating spoons on a soldier's helmet.

Jan Molenaer. *Two Boys and a Girl Making Music*. 1629. Oil on canvas. 68.3 x 84.5 cm (26 15/16 x 33 1/4"). National Gallery, London, United Kingdom.

Focus
- Describe the characteristics of Baroque music.
- Identify major influences of the time that still impact our lives today.

The Baroque Period— A Time of Elaboration

The **Baroque period** *(1600–1750)* was a time of great wealth and luxury for the royal and noble families of Europe. In the royal courts of the European kings, especially Louis XIV of France, life was a very fancy affair. Elaborate decoration was the rule in music, art, architecture, and fashion. Men and women of royalty wore wigs, high-heeled shoes, and colorful clothes decorated with costly lace. The term *baroque* comes from a French word meaning "imperfect or irregular pearls," which were used quite often as decorations on clothing of this period.

One of the reasons for the great wealth was the colonization of new lands with vast natural resources in the Americas and the Caribbean. In the early 1600s, groups from England, Germany and the Netherlands lived on the Eastern coast of what is today the United States. French and Spanish explorers were busily exploring and settling other parts of the New World.

With the new wealth came an interest in the arts and architecture. Royal and wealthy noble families sought to have the same level of access to art, music, and architecture that had been previously available primarily through the church.

A few of the great personalities of the Baroque period include:

- Johann Sebastian Bach—German composer
- Rembrandt van Rijn—Dutch painter
- John Milton—English writer
- William Harvey—English scientist who explained blood circulation
- Sir Isaac Newton—English scientist who formulated the theory of gravity

COMPOSERS
Johann Pachelbel (1653–1706)
Antonio Vivaldi (1678–1741)
Johann Sebastian Bach (1685–1750)
George Frideric Handel (1685–1759)

ARTISTS
El Greco (1541–1614)
Peter Paul Rubens (1577–1640)
Anthony van Dyck (1599–1641)
Rembrandt van Rijn (1606–1669)
Jan Vermeer (1632–1675)

AUTHORS
Ben Jonson (1572–1637)
René Descartes (1596–1650)
John Milton (1608–1674)
Molière (1622–1673)
Samuel Johnson (1709–1784)

VOCABULARY
Baroque period
oratorio
opera
concerto grosso
chorale

Baroque Music

The music of the Baroque period reflected the elaborate lifestyle of the time. Baroque composers wrote music that had great dramatic flair and a strong sense of movement. The melodies were often fancy and showy, but underneath them remained a clear and carefully planned musical structure.

Many new forms of vocal music were developed during the Baroque period. One new form was the **oratorio**, *a dramatic work for solo voices, chorus, and orchestra presented without theatrical action*. George Frideric Handel's (1685–1759) *Messiah* is an example of this form. Another form was the opera. An **opera** is *a combination of singing, instrumental music, dancing, and drama that tells a story*.

There was also a dramatic rise in importance of instrumental music. In earlier times, vocal music held dominance over instrumental music. Orchestras came into being with new forms of orchestral music. Composers created an independent instrumental style with dance suites, solo sonatas, solo concertos, overtures and fugues. A **concerto grosso** is *a multi-movement baroque piece for a group of soloists and an orchestra*. Two famous concertos grosso written during this time were Antonio Vivaldi's (1678–1741) *The Four Seasons* and Johann Sebastian Bach's (1685–1750) *Brandenburg Concertos*.

A number of instruments were developed during this time, including the clavichord, harpsichord, organ and clarinet.

Performance Links

When performing music of the Baroque period, it is important to apply the following guidelines:

- Sing with pitch accuracy, especially in chromatic sections.
- Identify which part has the dominant theme. Make sure that is heard over the accompaniment.
- When in the style of the piece, keep a steady, unrelenting pulse. Precision of dotted rhythms is especially important.
- Make any changes in dynamics at the same time in all parts.

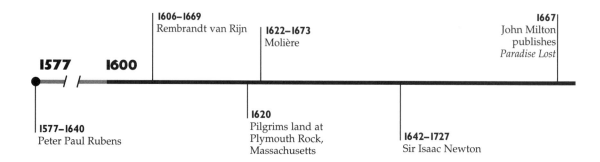

1577   1600

1606–1669
Rembrandt van Rijn

1622–1673
Molière

1667
John Milton
publishes
Paradise Lost

1577–1640
Peter Paul Rubens

1620
Pilgrims land at
Plymouth Rock,
Massachusetts

1642–1727
Sir Isaac Newton

Listening Links

CHORAL SELECTION
"Hallelujah Chorus" from *Messiah* by George Frideric Handel (1685–1759)

English composer George Frideric Handel was a musical genius. He often wrote music for special occasions for the nobility of England. Although Handel wrote operas, it was his oratorios that brought him lasting recognition. He wrote his most famous oratorio, *Messiah*, in twenty-four days.

The story has been told that King George I stood up during the first performance of "Hallelujah Chorus" to show his approval of the music. At that time, it was necessary for everyone to stand when the king was standing. Today, it is still customary to stand during the performance of this piece. The "Hallelujah Chorus" uses very few words. Identify the middle imitative section. Listen, and then write down the words that are used during this section.

INSTRUMENTAL SELECTION
Brandenburg Concerto No. 2, Third Movement by Johann Sebastian Bach (1685–1750)

German composer Johann Sebastian Bach was one of the greatest composers who ever lived. He came from a family of musicians, and learned to play the organ and the clavichord at an early age. A devout man of the Lutheran faith, Bach used **chorales**, or *hymn tunes*, in much of his sacred music. The quantity and quality of his music staggers the imagination.

Bach dedicated his six *Brandenburg Concertos* to the Margrave of Brandenburg in 1721. This selection features solo sections for trumpet, oboe, violin, and recorder. Describe what you hear during the solo sections.

Check Your Understanding

1. Compare and contrast oratorios and operas. Name one famous oratorio and its composer.

2. Describe characteristics of instrumental music during the Baroque period based on the *Brandenburg Concerto No. 2*, Third Movement.

3. Sir Isaac Newton discovered the law of gravity in the late 1600s. Discuss ways in which this discovery has influenced your life today.

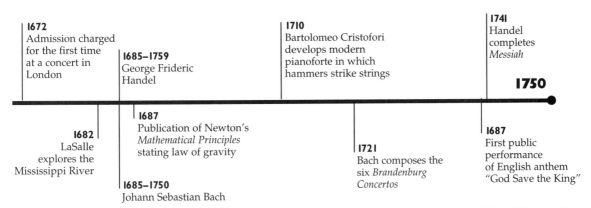

1672
Admission charged for the first time at a concert in London

1685–1759
George Frideric Handel

1710
Bartolomeo Cristofori develops modern pianoforte in which hammers strike strings

1741
Handel completes *Messiah*

1750

1682
LaSalle explores the Mississippi River

1687
Publication of Newton's *Mathematical Principles* stating law of gravity

1685–1750
Johann Sebastian Bach

1721
Bach composes the six *Brandenburg Concertos*

1687
First public performance of English anthem "God Save the King"

 Louis de Carmontelle (1717–1806) was a French architect, draftsman, painter, and printmaker. Although self-taught, Carmontelle drew hundreds of portraits that chronicle court life in France prior to the French Revolution. In this painting, Wolfgang Amadeus Mozart is seated at the piano performing music with his father, Leopold, and his sister, Nannerl. They are wearing the formal dress of the Classical period.

Louis de Carmontelle. *Leopold Mozart Making Music with Wolfgang and Nannerl.* c. 1763. Watercolor. Museé Conde, Chantilly, Paris, France.

Focus

- Identify two major composers from the Classical period.
- Describe characteristics of Classical music.

The Classical Period— A Time of Balance, Clarity, and Simplicity

The **Classical period** *(1750–1820)* was a time when people began looking to the early Greeks and Romans for order and structure in their lives. Artists and architects took note of the Greek and Roman objects being dug up in Athens, Pompeii, and other archeological sites. For example, the Arc de Triomphe in Paris, commissioned in 1806, was inspired by the Arch of Septiomus Severus in Rome.

The calm beauty and simplicity of this art from the past inspired artists and musicians to move away from the overly decorated styles of the Baroque period. The music, art, and architecture reflected a new emphasis on emotional restraint and simplicity.

The Classical period was witness to a rise in a democratic spirit in the lower and middle classes. Revolutions that took place in France and America abolished the rule by kings and queens, and established a more representative type of government. The main events in America during this period include the American Revolution (1775–1783), the signing of the Declaration of Independence (1776), the election of George Washington as the first President of the United States (1783), and the ratification of the National Constitution (1788).

Publishing increased dramatically, giving people other than the wealthy access to books and printed music. Among the famous books written during this period was Voltaire's *Candide*, which later served as the basis for a Broadway musical with music by Leonard Bernstein (1918–1990).

COMPOSERS

Carl Philipp Emanuel Bach
(1714–1788)

Johann Christian Bach
(1735–1762)

Franz Joseph Haydn
(1732–1809)

Wolfgang Amadeus Mozart
(1756–1791)

Ludwig van Beethoven
(1770–1827)

ARTISTS

Louis de Carmontelle
(1717–1806)

Thomas Gainsborough
(1727–1788)

Francisco Goya
(1746–1828)

Jacques-Louis David
(1748–1825)

Elisabeth Vigée-Lebrun
(1755–1842)

AUTHORS

Voltaire
(1694–1778)

William Wordsworth
(1770–1850)

Jane Austen
(1775–1817)

VOCABULARY

Classical period

secular music

homophony

crescendo

decrescendo

Music of the Classical Period

During the Classical period, people developed an interest in knowing more about the cultural aspects of life, such as art and music. One of the most important advances in the Classical period was the development of public concerts. Music was now written and performed for the general public, as well as for the royal courts and churches. The increasing popularity of public concerts led to a growth in the number of professional musicians and composers. For the first time, **secular music** (*music not associated with religious services or themes*) became the main type of music being formally composed.

The ideas of improvisation and exaggerated use of embellishments of the Baroque period were discarded. Music became simpler and more elegant, with a melody that sang out while the other parts provided a simple accompaniment. This type of music is known as **homophony**, or *music in which there are two or more parts with similar or identical rhythms being sung or played at the same time*. The two main composers associated with this period are Franz Joseph Haydn (1732–1809) and Wolfgang Amadeus Mozart (1756–1791). Their compositions were based on balance, clarity and simplicity. At the beginning of his career, Ludwig van Beethoven (1770–1827) also wrote music in the Classical style. Later, his style evolved into the more emotional and personal style of the Romantic period.

Performance Links

When performing music of the Classical period, it is important to apply the following guidelines:

- Listen for the melody line and do not allow the accompaniment parts to overshadow it.
- Sing chords in tune.
- Make gradual, not abrupt, dynamic changes. Move smoothly through each **crescendo** (*a dynamic marking that indicates to gradually sing louder*) and **decrescendo** (*a dynamic marking that indicates to gradually sing softer*).
- Keep phrases flowing and connected.

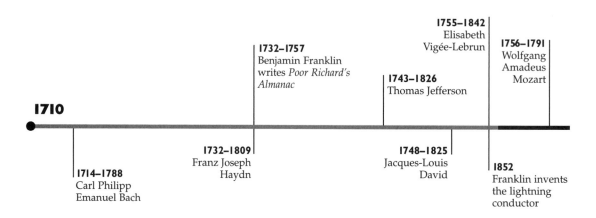

1710

1714–1788
Carl Philipp
Emanuel Bach

1732–1757
Benjamin Franklin
writes *Poor Richard's
Almanac*

1732–1809
Franz Joseph
Haydn

1743–1826
Thomas Jefferson

1748–1825
Jacques-Louis
David

1755–1842
Elisabeth
Vigée-Lebrun

1756–1791
Wolfgang
Amadeus
Mozart

1852
Franklin invents
the lightning
conductor

Listening Links

CHORAL SELECTION

"Confutatis" from *Requiem* by Wolfgang Amadeus Mozart (1756–1791)

Wolfgang Amadeus Mozart is recognized as one of the world's greatest composers. Born in Salzburg, Austria, Mozart was a child prodigy who had mastered the keyboard at age four and had written his first composition by age five.

Although Mozart died before completing the *Requiem*, the work was completed later by his student, Franz Süssmayer, and perhaps others. Mozart's *Requiem* has been performed and loved by many for over two centuries.

The "Confutatis" begins with an energetic rhythmic drive sung by the men's section and accompanied by a moving figure in the strings. The men's voices are interrupted twice. Identify what is happening musically during these interruptions. Describe how the piece ends.

INSTRUMENTAL SELECTION

Trumpet Concerto in E♭ Major, Third Movement by Franz Joseph Haydn (1732–1809)

Franz Joseph Haydn was another child prodigy from Austria. He introduced touches of folk and gypsy music into his works. Haydn, known as the "father of the symphony," composed over one hundred symphonies.

The *Trumpet Concerto in E♭ Major* was written in 1796 for Anton Weidinger, a friend of Haydn's who invented a trumpet with valves. The concerto was designed to demonstrate the flexibility of the new instrument. The opening theme is repeated numerous times. Listen to this piece and count the number of times you hear this theme.

Check Your Understanding

1. Name two important composers who wrote during the Classical period.

2. Analyze the main characteristics of Classical music as heard in *Requiem*: "Confutatis."

3. Describe how the Greek and Roman cultures influenced the Classical period.

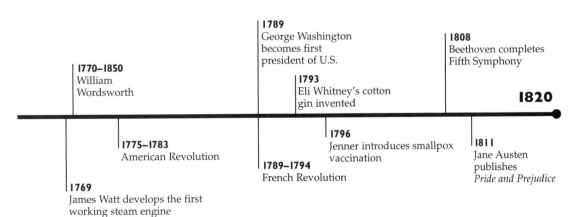

1789
George Washington becomes first president of U.S.

1808
Beethoven completes Fifth Symphony

1770–1850
William Wordsworth

1793
Eli Whitney's cotton gin invented

1820

1775–1783
American Revolution

1796
Jenner introduces smallpox vaccination

1811
Jane Austen publishes *Pride and Prejudice*

1789–1794
French Revolution

1769
James Watt develops the first working steam engine

Pierre-Auguste Renoir (1841–1919) was a French impressionist who focused on people in informal gatherings. Often, their actions were important, even though there was not always an obvious suggestion of the story. His paintings captured the relationship among his subjects and their feelings. He enjoyed showing the joyful side of life.

Pierre-Auguste Renoir. *Two Young Girls at the Piano.* 1892. Oil on canvas. 111.8 x 86.4 cm (44 x 34"). The Metropolitan Museum of Art, New York, New York. Robert Lehman Collection.

Focus
• Describe cultural events of the Romantic period.
• Describe characteristics of Romantic music.

The Romantic Period—
A Time of Drama

The **Romantic period** *(1820–1900)* was a period when composers wrote music that was filled with emotion. It was, in many ways, a reaction against the Classical period (1750–1820), when music was based on emotional restraint and formal structure.

The Romantic period was a time of tremendous change in the world. Scientific and mechanical achievements led to advances in transportation (steamboats, railways), communication (telegraph, telephone), and manufacturing (steel production, food canning). There was a move from living on farms to working in the factories. These changes helped to bring about the Industrial Revolution.

The Industrial Revolution produced a wealthy middle class. Their new wealth provided music for the masses to a far greater degree than had existed before. Musicians' incomes were now generated by the sale of concert tickets and published music rather than by the patronage of the church or the very wealthy. By not being associated with a patron, composers could show more individualism and freedom in their writing.

Visual artists of the Romantic period began to explore the world around them. They painted nature scenes, and focused on natural light in these scenes. In France, such artists were known as Impressionists; they included Edouard Manet, Edgar Degas, Pierre Renoir, and the sculptor Auguste Rodin.

Writers of the time told tales of adventure (*The Three Musketeers* by Alexandre Dumas, *Tom Sawyer* by Mark Twain), the changes in society (*Oliver Twist* by Charles Dickens), and exotic places (*Jungle Book* by Rudyard Kipling). Science fiction also became a popular theme of stories (*20,000 Leagues Under the Sea* by Jules Verne).

COMPOSERS
Ludwig van Beethoven (1770–1827)
Franz Schubert (1797–1828)
Felix Mendelssohn (1809–1847)
Frédéric Chopin (1810–1849)
Franz Liszt (1811–1886)
Richard Wagner (1813–1883)
Giuseppe Verdi (1813–1901)
Johannes Brahms (1833–1897)
Georges Bizet (1838–1875)
Peter Ilyich Tchaikovsky (1840–1893)
Antonín Dvořák (1841–1904)
Claude Debussy (1862–1918)

ARTISTS
Edouard Manet (1832–1883)
Edgar Degas (1834–1917)
Paul Cezanne (1839–1906)
Auguste Rodin (1840–1917)
Claude Monet (1840–1926)
Pierre-Auguste Renoir (1841–1919)
Mary Cassatt (1845–1926)
Paul Gauguin (1848–1903)
Vincent van Gogh (1853–1890)

AUTHORS
Alexandre Dumas (1802–1870)
Henry Wadsworth Longfellow (1807–1882)
Charles Dickens (1812–1870)
Jules Verne (1828–1905)
Louisa May Alcott (1832–1884)
Mark Twain (1835–1910)
Rudyard Kipling (1865–1905)

VOCABULARY
Romantic period
opera
mass
requiem

Music of the Romantic Period

Composers of the Romantic period created music that was full of emotion and less structured than music of the Classical period. Melodies became longer and more expressive, and harmonies became more colorful. Larger orchestras were used to expand the available sounds in the music. Creativity was enhanced as the rules of composition were relaxed or broken.

Romantic music reflected the period's spirit of nationalism. Richard Wagner (1813–1883) highlighted German music and legends in his operas, while Giuseppe Verdi (1813–1901) wrote operas that preserved the historical and cultural traditions of his native Italy. Upon a visit to the United States, Antonin Dvorák (1841–1904), a Czech composer, wrote his famous *Symphony from the New World* to describe America.

Other composers focused on stories in works such as Modest Mussorgsky's (1839–1881) *Night on Bald Mountain* and Georges Bizet's (1838–1875) *Carmen*. Still others, like Claude Debussy (1862–1918), joined the Impressionist movement and wrote music that suggested scenes or feelings. Ludwig van Beethoven (1770–1827) crossed the bridge between the Classical and Romantic periods. His later music exhibited the emotion, rhythm, and disregard for form that was characteristic of the Romantics.

One composer most associated with the Romantic movement is Frédéric Chopin (1810–1849). His piano music explored a wide variety of strong and quiet emotions. Other composers of the period include Peter Ilyich Tchaikovsky (1840–1893) whose *Nutcracker Suite* is a staple of Christmas celebrations, and Johannes Brahms (1833–1897) whose *Lullaby* is still sung to young children across the globe.

Performance Links

When performing music of the Romantic period, it is important to apply the following guidelines:

- Perform accurately the wide range of dynamics and tempos.
- Concentrate on phrasing, making the connection between the words and the music.
- Sing with confidence in foreign languages to reflect nationalism in music.

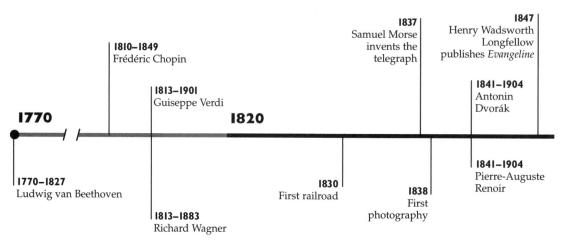

Listening Links

CHORAL SELECTION

"Dies Irae" from *Requiem* by Giuseppe Verdi (1813–1901)

Giuseppe Verdi, a famous Italian composer, wrote twenty-six operas and several other works. An **opera** is *a combination of singing, instrumental music, dancing and drama that tells a story.* When Verdi died, the streets of Milan, Italy, were filled with thousands of mourners, who followed his coffin through the streets singing a chorus from one of his operas.

A **mass** is *a religious service of prayers and ceremonies.* Originating in the Roman Catholic Church it consists of spoken and sung sections. Sometimes a special mass known as a **requiem**, or *a mass for the dead,* is used. "Dies Irae" is one section of the Verdi *Requiem* that was first performed in 1874. Describe the opening section of this piece.

INSTRUMENTAL SELECTION

"Ride of the Valkyries" from *Die Walkure* by Richard Wagner (1813–1883)

Richard Wagner was a German composer whose composing style was very expressive. His music often painted a picture, and was on the grandest scale. His work greatly influenced future composers.

Wagner's *Die Walkure* is an opera based on a legend from Norse mythology. It tells the story of Wotan, the leader of the gods, who had nine daughters called Valkyries, or warrior maidens. Wotan ordered the Valkyries to bring him the world's bravest heroes, whom he would then transform into immortals to protect the gods. Act Three begins with the "Ride of the Valkyries," a scene where the warrior maidens gallop through a storm carrying the brave heroes to Valhalla, the mountaintop home of the gods. As you listen to "Ride of the Valkyries," identify when and where you have heard this music before.

Check Your Understanding

1. Name two Romantic compositions and their composers.

2. Compare musical characteristics of the Classical and Romantic periods.

3. Discuss influences on your life today that originated during the Romantic period.

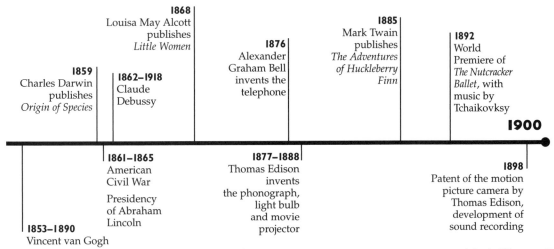

1868
Louisa May Alcott publishes *Little Women*

1876
Alexander Graham Bell invents the telephone

1885
Mark Twain publishes *The Adventures of Huckleberry Finn*

1892
World Premiere of *The Nutcracker Ballet*, with music by Tchaikovksy

1859
Charles Darwin publishes *Origin of Species*

1862–1918
Claude Debussy

1900

1861–1865
American Civil War

Presidency of Abraham Lincoln

1877–1888
Thomas Edison invents the phonograph, light bulb and movie projector

1898
Patent of the motion picture camera by Thomas Edison, development of sound recording

1853–1890
Vincent van Gogh

 *Fallingwater* is one of the most inventive houses built by Frank Lloyd Wright (1867–1959). Surrounding foliage and waterfalls merge the architecture with nature. Walls are avoided almost entirely, allowing the overhangs to provide a sense of shelter.

Frank Lloyd Wright. *Fallingwater*. Bear Run, Pennsylvania. 1936. The Frank Lloyd Wright Foundation, Scottsdale, Arizona.

Focus

- Identify the major twentieth century influences on music.
- Describe characteristics of Contemporary music.

The Contemporary Period— A Time of Change

The change from nineteenth century Romanticism to twenty-first century Modernism is as dramatic as comparing horse-drawn carriages to the rockets of the space age. The world has moved fast, and change has been constant.

New scientific discoveries and inventions began with the Industrial Revolution in the late 1800s and have continued to the present day. Technological advances were accelerated during World War I (1914–1918) and World War II (1939–1945). These advances have produced such things as the airplane, radio, television, jet propulsion, radar, atomic energy, computers and the Internet, and the exploration of outer space.

The world has become "smaller" because new technologies have made it possible to learn about world events. One can visit other parts of the world and other peoples in far less time. New ideas, sounds and trends can spread worldwide almost instantaneously.

Individualism, the principle of independent thought, combined with technology has provided artists, writers and composers with new ideas and materials for their creative endeavors. Artists such as Pablo Picasso rebelled against tradition and began to create works that were abstract. His works often did not represent objects in nature as they appeared to the eye. Some writers began to write fewer plot-driven stories and focus more on people and their thoughts and feelings.

COMPOSERS

Sergei Rachmaninoff (1873–1943)
Arnold Schoenberg (1874–1951)
Béla Bartók (1881–1945)
Igor Stravinsky (1882–1971)
Sergey Prokofiev (1891–1953)
Carl Orff (1895–1982)
Aaron Copland (1900–1990)
Benjamin Britten (1913–1976)
Leonard Bernstein (1918–1990)
John Williams (1932–)

ARTISTS

Henri Matisse (1869–1954)
Pablo Picasso (1881–1973)
Wassily Kandinsky (1866–1944)
Marc Chagall (1887–1985)
Georgia O'Keeffe (1887–1986)
Andy Warhol (1930–1987)

AUTHORS

Robert Frost (1874–1963)
Virginia Woolf (1882–1941)
Ernest Hemingway (1899–1961)
Rachel Carson (1907–1964)
James Baldwin (1924–1997)
JK Rowling (b. 1965)

VOCABULARY

synthesizer
dissonance
improvisation
fugue

Music of the Contemporary Period

A great deal of change occurred in music during the late twentieth century. Technology had a large influence on these changes. Record, cassette tape and CD players made music readily available to everyone. Radios and televisions brought live music performances into people's homes. Often, acoustic instruments were replaced by the **synthesizer,** *a musical instrument that produces sounds electronically, rather than by physical vibrations.*

Like abstract art, music of this time has sought to shed itself of the musical conventions of melody, harmony, and rhythm adhered to in previous periods. Composers began to use different scales, such as Arnold Schoenberg's (1874–1951) twelve-tone system, different and complex rhythms, as in Igor Stravinsky's (1882–1971) works, and different harmonies as used by Bela Bartók (1881–1945). It was not uncommon for audiences to find this music unpleasant to the ear and filled with **dissonance** *(a combination of tones that clash).*

A new symphony form was introduced in which narrative accompanied the music. Most popular was Sergei Prokofiev's (1891–1953) *Peter and the Wolf.* Classical composers such as Aaron Copland were sought to provide music for motion pictures and ballet. Leopold Stokowski, a famous conductor, worked with Walt Disney to create the animated film *Fantasia,* based on classical music. John Williams (b. 1932), a more contemporary composer of orchestral works, has become world-famous for his themes for movies such as *Jaws* and *Star Wars.*

Performance Links

When performing music of the Contemporary period, it is important to apply the following guidelines:

- Sing on pitch, even in extreme parts of your range.
- Tune intervals carefully in the wide skips found in many melodic lines.
- Perform changing meters and unusual rhythm patterns precisely.
- Observe accurately the wide range in dynamics and tempos.

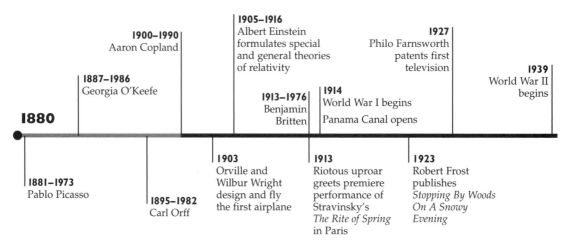

CHORAL SELECTION
"O Fortuna" from *Carmina Burana* by Carl Orff (1895–1982)

Carl Orff was a German composer, perhaps best known for developing a creative approach to music education that involves speech, moving, singing, playing instruments and **improvisation** *(the art of singing or playing music, making it up as you go).*

Carmina Burana, sung in Latin and German, uses the texts from twenty-five ancient poems and love songs that were popular during the Middle Ages. It is written for solo singers, chorus and orchestra. Composed in 1937, *Carmina Burana* opens and closes with the "O Fortuna" chorus. Its text implies that life is unpredictable and fate is fickle. Orff's music often features exciting rhythms and insistent repeated note patterns. Listen for the repeated note pattern in "O Fortuna."

INSTRUMENTAL SELECTION
"Fugue" from *A Young Person's Guide to the Orchestra* by Benjamin Britten (1913–1976)

The English composer Benjamin Britten was a child genius. At the age of two, he begged his mother to teach him to play the piano. By age 16, he had composed a symphony and many other works. Benjamin Britten was highly regarded around the world, and in 1963 he was honored as England's Composer of the Year.

A Young Person's Guide to the Orchestra was written in 1945 to teach students about the instruments of the orchestra. Britten uses a fugue to highlight each section of the orchestra, and then combines them for a grand ending. A **fugue** is *a form of imitation in which a melody is performed by different instruments, entering at different times, thus adding layers of sound.* Identify each solo instrument or section as they enter.

Check Your Understanding

1. Name two important Contemporary period composers and describe their music.

2. Analyze the complex rhythms heard in "O Fortuna."

3. Summarize the changes that have made music more accessible during the twentieth century. Discuss how technology has influenced this change.

1945
First atomic bomb
dropped on Hiroshima

United Nations
organized

1969
First manned lunar
landing by the
United States

1989
Englishman Timothy
Berner-Lee introduces
the World Wide Web,
allowing universal
access to the Internet

present

1957
First satellite,
Sputnik I,
launched into
space by the
Soviet Union

1972
Robert Moog
patents the
Moog synthesizer

Concert Etiquette

The term **concert etiquette** describes *how we are expected to behave in formal musical performances.* Understanding appropriate concert etiquette allows you to be considerate of others, including audience members and performers. It also helps everyone attending to enjoy the performance.

Different types of musical performances dictate certain behavior guidelines. How one shows excitement at a rock concert is certainly worlds apart from the appropriate behavior at a formal concert or theater production. Understanding these differences allows audience members to behave in a manner that shows consideration and respect for everyone involved.

What are the expectations of a good audience member at a formal musical presentation?

- Arrive on time. If you arrive after the performance has begun, wait outside the auditorium until a break in the music to enter the hall.

- Remain quiet and still during the performance. Talking and moving around prevent others from hearing and enjoying the performance.

- Leave the auditorium only in case of an emergency. Try to leave during a break in the musical selections.

- Sing or clap along only when invited to do so by the performers or the conductor.

- Applaud at the end of a composition or when the conductor's arms are lowered at the conclusion of a performance. It is customary to not applaud between movements or sections of a major work.

- Save shouting, whistling and dancing for rock concerts or athletic events. These are never appropriate at formal musical performances.

Remembering these important behavior guidelines will ensure that everyone enjoys the show!

Choral Library

An American Folk Song Spectacular!

Composer: American Folk Songs, arranged by John Leavitt
Text: Traditional
Voicing: 2-Part

Focus

- Read and perform rhythmic patterns with eighth notes.
- Identify by ear and notate melodic patterns.
- Use dramatic storytelling to interpret musical content.

 **SPOTLIGHT**

To learn more about arranging, see page 20.

Getting Started

If you could pack your bags and take off tomorrow, where would you go? The call of the open road is hard to resist. Throughout the history of the American West, pioneers, cowboys, and prospectors hit the trail looking for adventure and new fortunes.

Singing and dancing have always been an important part of the American West. Not only did music lift the spirits of the pioneers, but the songs they created became records of their adventures.

◆ History and Culture

"An American Folk Song Spectacular!" is a **medley,** or *a collection of songs musically linked together.* The four selections in this medley are examples of American folk songs. **Folk songs** are *songs that have been passed down through oral tradition and often describe a certain place or event.*

The melody to "The Red River Valley," though popular with the American cowboy, originated in New York State. After the Civil War, the Chisholm Trail provided a direct route for the longhorn cattle from Texas, through Oklahoma, to the railhead at Abilene, Kansas. Composed in the 1840s, Stephen Foster's "Oh! Susanna" was popular with the gold-seeking 49ers. "Skip to My Lou," a play-party dance, was a favorite among young people.

Links to Learning

◆ Vocal

Read and perform the following examples to establish the key of G major.

1

do mi sol mi do

2

do sol do

"An American Folk Song Spectacular!" begins in the key of G major and is based on the G major scale. To locate "G" on a piano, find any set of three black keys. "G" is the white key to the left of the middle black key. This scale uses the notes G, A, B, C, D, E, F♯, G. Using the keyboard below as a guide, play the G major scale.

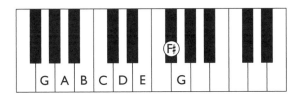

Sing the G major scale.

G	A	B	C	D	E	F♯	G	F♯	E	D	C	B	A	G
do	re	mi	fa	sol	la	ti	do	ti	la	sol	fa	mi	re	do

◆ Theory

Perform the following rhythmic pattern in $\frac{4}{4}$ **meter**, *a time signature in which there are four beats per measure and the quarter note receives the beat.*

◆ Artistic Expression

The cowboy sings, "I'll tell you of my troubles on the old Chisholm Trail." What troubles might he be speaking of? Imagine you are that cowboy in 1870. Write a letter to your family back home about your adventures on the Chisholm Trail.

Evaluation

Demonstrate how well you have learned the skills and concepts featured in the lesson "An American Folksong Spectacular!" by completing the following:

- Using the notes *do, mi,* and *sol,* create a four-note melodic pattern in the key of G major. Sing your pattern on "loo" and ask a classmate to identify the notes that you've sung. Have the classmate write the four notes on manuscript paper. Switch roles.
- In the character of the cowboy, present your Chisholm Trail letter to the class.

An American Folk Song Spectacular!

The Red River Valley • The Old Chisholm Trail • Oh! Susanna • Skip To My Lou

For 2-Part and Piano

Arranged by
JOHN LEAVITT

American Folk Songs

THE RED RIVER VALLEY
Traditional American Cowboy Song
Slowly, with feeling (♩ = ca. 63)

*Close to "n," sustaining.

THE OLD CHISHOLM TRAIL

[8] Traditional American Cowboy Song
Brightly! (♩ = ca. 138)

while. *(solo shout)* **He - Hah!** Well,

while. Well,

[12] come a - long boys and lis - ten to my tale, I'll

come a - long boys and lis - ten to my tale, I'll

tell you of my trou - bles on the old Chis - holm Trail. My

tell you of my trou - bles on the old Chis - holm Trail.

*Click click *etc.*

27

up in the morn-in' be - fore day - light, *Click click

and be -

click *(etc.)* I'll ride my horse to the

fore I sleep the moon shines bright. I'll ride my horse to the

* *Tongue clicks in alternating pitches*

top of the hill. I'll work all day, you know I will. Co-ma

top of the hill. I'll work all day, you know I will. Co-ma

35

ti - yi you-py yap-py yay, yap-py yay, co-ma

ti - yi you-py yap-py yay, yap-py yay, co-ma

ti - yi you-py yap-py yay.

ti - yi you-py yap-py yay.

OH! SUSANNA

40 **Words and Music by Stephen Collins Foster**
Dance-like (♩ = ca. 120)

goin' to Loui - si - a - na my ____ true love for to see.

goin' to Loui - si - a - na my ____ true love for to see.

End whistle All sing

Oh! Su - san - na, oh, don't you cry for me, I've ____

End whistle All sing

Oh! Su - san - na, oh, don't you cry for me, I've ____

come from A - la - ba - ma with my ban - jo on my knee.

come from A - la - ba - ma with my ban - jo on my knee.

54

(♪ = ♪)

Oh! Su - san - na. _____

Oh! Su - san - na. _____

8vb ⌐

59 SKIP TO MY LOU
Traditional
mf

Optional 1st Solo

Lou, *clap clap* Lou, *clap clap*

8va - - - - - - - - - - - - - - - - - - -

mf

8vb ⌐

skip to my Lou,

Optional 2nd Solo *mf*

Lou, *clap clap* Lou, *clap clap*

Blues, Blues, Blues

Composer: Kirby Shaw
Text: Kirby Shaw
Voicing: 2-Part

VOCABULARY

blues style

blues scale

call and response

swing rhythms

improvisation

SPOTLIGHT

To learn more about improvisation, see page 147.

Focus

• Compose and perform rhythmic patterns in swing style

• Perform music that represents the blues style

Getting Started

Blues style is *an original African American art form that developed in the early twentieth century in the Mississippi Delta region of the South.* The lyrics of these songs often express feelings of frustration, hardship, or longing. The best-known early blues performers include Ma Rainey, Bessie Smith and Billie Holiday. Today, the blues influence can be heard in the music of B. B. King, Susan Tedeschi and Keb'Mo'.

◆ History and Culture

Characteristics of the blues style found in "Blues, Blues, Blues" include the blues scale, call and response, and swing rhythms. The **blues scale** is *an altered major scale with lowered or flatted notes.* These flatted notes, often called the blue notes, appear in much African American music and reflect the African influence. Call and response comes from the field hollers used by slaves as they worked. In **call and response**, *a leader or group sings a phrase (call), followed by the response to that phrase by another group.* **Swing rhythms** are *rhythms made by changing two even eighth notes into two uneven eighth notes.* The first note becomes longer than the second, and a triplet feel is created. "Blues, Blues, Blues" should be performed in the swing style.

Another common characteristic of the blues style is the use of **improvisation**, or *the art of singing or playing music, making it up as you go.* It may take practice to develop this skill, but improvisation can be a lot of fun.

Links to Learning

◆ Vocal

Perform the following examples to practice singing major and blues scales. Discuss the differences in the two.

◆ Theory

Read and perform the following rhythmic pattern. As you perform, move your arms and upper body in a dance-like style that reflects the triplet motion.

Read and perform this new rhythmic pattern. Continue to move your arms and upper body in the triplet style.

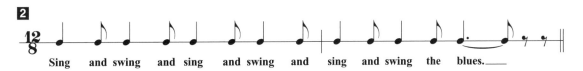

Now read this rhythmic pattern as even eighth notes, but perform the pattern in a swing style. Exercises 2 and 3 should sound the same. Continue to move as you perform.

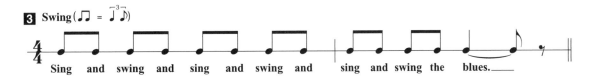

Evaluation

Demonstrate how well you have learned the skills and concepts featured in the lesson "Blues, Blues, Blues" by completing the following:

- Compose an eight-beat rhythmic pattern in $\frac{4}{4}$ meter that includes eighth notes. Perform the pattern first using even eighth notes and then again using uneven, or swing, eighth notes.

- As you sing "Blues, Blues, Blues" from memory, step or walk the beat in a dance-like manner. Demonstrate the triplet or swing feel in your movement.

Blues, Blues, Blues

For 2-Part and Piano

Words and Music by
KIRBY SHAW

now we're sing - in' the blues, __

- in' the blues, __ now we're sing -

now we're sing - in' the blues, __ we're as

- in' the blues, now we're sing - in' the blues, __ we're as

blue__ as blue can be! __ Oh yeah!

blue__ as blue can be! __ Oh yeah!

SPOTLIGHT

Improvisation

Blues style is *an original African American art form that developed in the early twentieth century in the South.* One characteristic of the blues style is call and response. In **call and response,** *a leader or group sings a phrase (call), followed by the response to that phrase by another group.* Another common characteristic of the blues style is the use of **improvisation,** or *the art of singing or playing music, making it up as you go.* Blues performers often improvise their music as they perform.

By using call and response, you can learn the first step toward improvisation.

As a class, read and perform the following call:

Call

I'm sing - in' the blues.

Read and perform the following responses:

Response 1

Yes, you're sing - in' the blues.

Response 2

Yes, you're sing-in', sing - in' the blues.

Response 3

Yes, oh yes, you're sing - in' the blues.

As the class sings the call, take turns individually singing one of the three responses. Now you are ready to make up your own responses. Improvise!

Brand New Day

Composer: Cristi Cary Miller
Text: Angela Darter Stogsdill
Voicing: 2-Part

 **SPOTLIGHT**

To learn more about vocal production, see page 63.

Focus

- Extend the vocal range.
- Sing with expression.
- Perform music in major tonality.

Getting Started

Have you ever liked a tune so well that you could not get it out of your mind? Have you ever found yourself singing or humming the same tune all day long? "Brand New Day" is that kind of song. With its catchy melody and snappy rhythms, this song is bound to stay with you for a long time.

◆ History and Culture

You have often heard the phrases "dare to dream," "seize the day," and "reach for the stars." These ideas promote a positive outlook on life. They support the attitude that if we dare to dream and strive to make those dreams come true, we will find joy and purpose in our lives.

Follow your dreams and be on your way.

Start with a smile! It's a brand new day!

Scientific research has shown that music affects us physically and mentally in a positive way. Music helps develop the human mind and spirit. It allows us to express feelings and ideas in a unique way. In this song, the messages of happiness and new beginnings are conveyed from you, the performer, to the audience through the medium of music. You can share this message with your audience through your enthusiasm, the excited expression on your face, and your singing posture. These elements combine to create your overall stage presence. Let everyone see your joy in making music.

Links to Learning

◆ Vocal

Perform the following example to develop, and to practice singing in, your **head voice,** or *the higher part of your singing range.*

lah———————— lah——————— (etc.)

◆ Theory

"Brand New Day" begins in the key of B♭ major and is based on the B♭ major scale. *A song that is based on a major scale with "do" as its keynote, or home tone, is described as* being in **major tonality**. To locate "B♭" on a piano, find any set of three black keys. "B♭" is the top black key. This scale uses the notes B♭, C, D, E♭, F, G, A, B♭. Using the keyboard below as a guide, play the B♭ major scale.

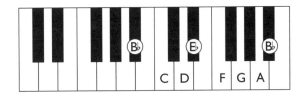

Sing the B♭ major scale.

| B♭ | C | D | E♭ | F | G | A | B♭ | A | G | F | E♭ | D | C | B♭ |
| do | re | mi | fa | sol | la | ti | do | ti | la | sol | fa | mi | re | do |

Evaluation

Demonstrate how well you have learned the skills and concepts featured in the lesson "Brand New Day" by completing the following:

- Sing the vocal example above. With the help of your teacher, find the highest note in your own vocal range that can be sung relaxed, sustained, and with accurate pitch.

- Sing measures 9–17 alone or with others to show how you can express the meaning of the text through your overall stage presence.

Brand New Day

For 2-Part and Piano

Words by
ANGELA DARTER STOGSDILL

Music by
CRISTI CARY MILLER

Consider Yourself

Composer: Lionel Bart, arranged by John Leavitt
Text: Lionel Bart
Voicing: 2-Part

VOCABULARY

half step

chromatic scale

simple meter

compound meter

 SPOTLIGHT

To learn more about concert etiquette, see page 126.

Focus

- Sing chromatic pitches accurately.
- Read and write music notation in compound meter.

Getting Started

"Consider Yourself," from the musical *Oliver!*, is an energetic song that extends an invitation to feel "at home" and to be "one of the family." In the story, Oliver is an orphan who has been thrown out of a poorhouse for being bold enough to ask for more food. On his own in London, he meets a gang of pickpockets who live on the streets. The young thieves welcome Oliver into their group by singing "Consider Yourself." In the end, Oliver is rescued by a kind gentleman who turns out to be his grandfather.

◆ History and Culture

Do you have a favorite television show that you enjoy watching every week? Do you know all the characters by name? Do you know the plot lines? Before television, ongoing stories appeared in magazines. Like episodes of a TV show, each issue featured a new chapter.

Oliver! is based on the novel *Oliver Twist,* by the British author Charles Dickens (1812–1870). The story was originally issued in 24 installments from 1837–1839. Later, it was published as a book. Dickens wrote numerous novels and stories, the best-known being the holiday favorite *A Christmas Carol.*

Links to Learning

◆ Vocal

A **half step** is *the smallest distance between two notes.* A **chromatic scale** is *a scale that consists of all half steps.* Perform the following example to practice singing chromatically or by half steps.

◆ Theory

There are two general categories of meter: simple meter and compound meter. In **simple meter,** *the quarter note receives the beat, and the division of the beat is based on two eighth notes.* $\frac{4}{4}$ $\frac{3}{4}$, and $\frac{2}{4}$ are examples of simple meter. In **compound meter,** *the dotted quarter note receives the beat, and the division of the beat is based on three eighth notes.* $\frac{6}{8}$ meter is an example of compound meter.

Like $\frac{2}{4}$, $\frac{6}{8}$ meter is usually counted in two (except when the tempo is very slow). Read and perform the following examples to practice reading rhythmic patterns in compound meter.

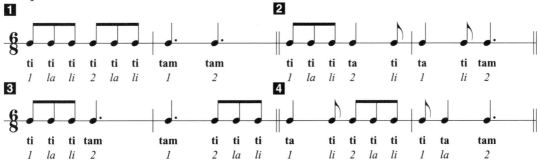

◆ Artistic Expression

To develop artistry through expressive singing, form a group of three to five singers. Ask one member of the group to observe facial expressions while the others sing the song. Identify expressions that communicate the invitation presented in the lyrics.

Evaluation

Demonstrate how well you have learned the skills and concepts featured in the lesson "Consider Yourself" by completing the following:

- Perform your part from measures 13–29 to demonstrate your ability to sing chromatically.

- Using the rhythmic patterns found in the Theory section above as a guide, create your own four-measure pattern in compound meter. Perform your composition for the class.

From the Broadway Show OLIVER!

Consider Yourself

For 2-Part and Piano

Arranged by
JOHN LEAVITT

Words and Music by
LIONEL BART

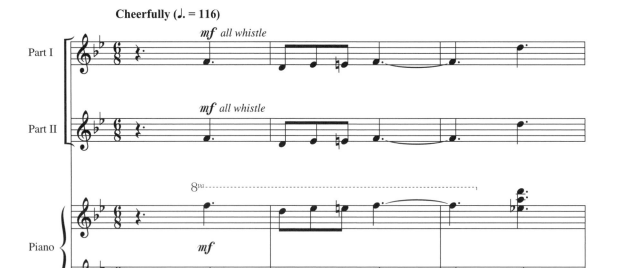

con - sid - er your-self____ one of the fam - i - ly.

We've tak-en to you____ so strong,

it's clear, we're go-ing to get a-

sid - er your - self _____ our mate.   We

don't want to have _____ no fuss,

2nd time to CODA ⊕ (m. 96)

end whistle *subito* ***p***   *cresc.*

for   af - ter some con - sid - er - a - tion

end whistle *subito* ***p***   *cresc.*

subito ***p***   *cresc.*

we can state: "Con - sid - er your - self   one   of

us."

Hine ma tov

Composer: Hebrew Folk Song, arranged by Henry Leck
Text: Traditional
Voicing: 2-Part

VOCABULARY

minor tonality
$\frac{2}{4}$ meter

Focus

- Perform music in minor tonality.
- Compose rhythmic phrases.
- Perform music that represents the Hebrew culture.

SKILL BUILDERS

To learn more about the key of E minor, see Beginning Sight-Singing, *page 94.*

Getting Started

Imagine that you are at a festive occasion. Perhaps it is a celebration such as a wedding, a birthday party, or a bar mitzvah. You hear the host ask the guests to come join in a dance. The people begin to sing and dance in a circle while holding hands or interlocking arms. "Hine ma tov" is the type of song that might be performed for this occasion.

◆ History and Culture

People have always danced as a means of expression. This is particularly true in Israel. Despite the fact that its people have a heritage that spans thousands of years, Israel did not achieve statehood until 1948.

Over the years, Jewish people have developed a rich tradition of folk art, music, and dance. "Hine ma tov" is an example of this rich heritage. The English translation is: "Behold, how good and pleasant it is for brethren to dwell together in unity."

On page 232 in this book you will find the lesson "Unity." Although "Unity" is written in the African American gospel tradition, it uses the same text as "Hine ma tov." Listen to both songs and discuss the ways in which two different cultures have chosen to express a similar theme of unity and peace.

Links to Learning

◆ Vocal

"Hine ma tov" begins in the key of E minor and is based on the E minor scale. *A song that is based on a minor scale with* la *as its keynote, or home tone, is described as being* in **minor tonality**. Sing the E minor scale.

E	F♯	G	A	B	C	D	E	D	C	B	A	G	F♯	E
la	ti	do	re	mi	fa	sol	la	sol	fa	mi	re	do	ti	la

Read and perform the following examples to practice singing some of the melodic patterns found in "Hine ma tov."

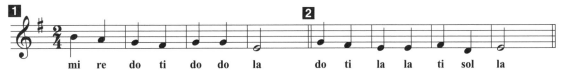

◆ Theory

Read and speak the following rhythmic patterns. Silently mouth the syllables in parentheses to help feel the space needed for the longer note values. To develop a strong sense of two beats per measure, put extra emphasis on the word "boom" each time it occurs. **²⁄₄ meter** is *a time signature in which there are two beats per measure and the quarter note receives the beat.*

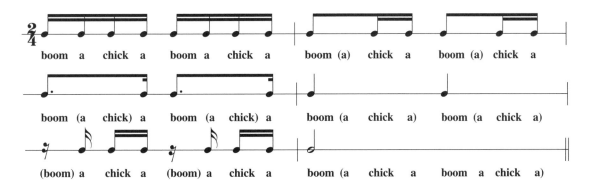

Evaluation

Demonstrate how well you have learned the skills and concepts featured in the lesson "Hine ma tov" by completing the following:

- Sing measures 5–20 to show that you can sing in minor tonality.

- Compose a four-measure rhythmic composition in ²⁄₄ meter using the rhythms presented in this lesson. Perform your composition for the class.

Hine ma tov

For 2-Part and Piano

Arranged by
HENRY LECK

Hebrew Folk Song

La la la la la la la la   la la la la la   la

La la la la la la la la   la la la la la   Hi -

SPOTLIGHT

Careers In Music

Composer/Arranger

Composers turn their ideas into music just as authors write original stories and artists paint original pieces of art. A **composer** is *a person who takes a musical thought and writes it out in musical notation to share with others.* There are no special degree requirements to be a composer, but a thorough knowledge of music and music technology is helpful. Some composers write their music with the use of a MIDI and music software on the computer. Others write their music compositions out by hand on manuscript paper.

Composing is a very competitive field. Some composers are able to make a good living from writing, but not all. It depends on whether there is a demand for the type of music they write and whether they have connections with those who can get it published.

As a young aspiring composer, it is necessary for you to listen to as much variety of music as possible, including classical, jazz, world music, and popular. Broaden your musical knowledge. Study the music of the composers you really like. Begin by emulating their style, then branch out to create your own style. Look for ways to make your compositions unique.

Also, composers may use their talents to write arrangements of existing tunes. An **arranger** is *a composer who takes an original or existing melody and adds extra features or changes the melody in some way.* Look through the songs in this book and find one example of an original composition and one example of an arrangement.

Little David, Play On Your Harp

Composer: African American Spiritual, arranged by Emily Crocker
Text: Traditional
Voicing: 2-Part

VOCABULARY

syncopation

spiritual

imitation

descant

Focus

- Define *imitation.*
- Identify and perform syncopated and non-syncopated rhythms.
- Perform music that represents the African American spiritual.

 **SKILL BUILDERS**

To learn more about sixteenth and eighth note combinations, see Beginning Sight-Singing, page 74.

Getting Started

Imagine yourself at a football game. The cheerleaders are cheering the team to victory, and the band is playing the fight song. The unique rhythms that you hear grab your attention and encourage you to move to the beat. This excitement in the music is caused by syncopation. **Syncopation** occurs when *the accent is moved from a strong beat to a weak beat or the weak portion of a beat.* Enjoy singing the many syncopated rhythms in "Little David, Play On Your Harp."

◆ History and Culture

"Little David, Play On Your Harp" is an example of a spiritual. A part of the African American tradition, **spirituals** are *songs that are often based on biblical themes or stories and were first sung by the slaves.* What spirituals do you know?

In this arrangement, two musical devices—imitation and descant—are used to create interest and variety. **Imitation** occurs when *one part copies what the other part has just sung.* A **descant** is *a special part that is added to the other parts in a song and is usually sung higher than the other parts.* Find examples of imitation, and locate the descant in this song.

Links to Learning

◆ Vocal

Perform the following example below to practice singing intervals found in "Little David, Play On Your Harp."

la   la   la   la   la   la   la   la   la   la   la   la   la   la   la   la   la   la   la   la

◆ Theory

Read and perform the following syncopated and non-syncopated rhythmic patterns used in "Little David, Play On Your Harp."

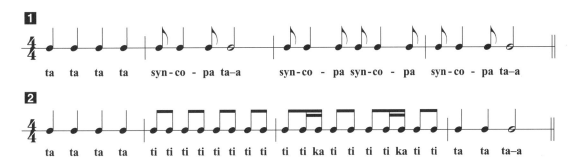

1

ta   ta   ta   ta   syn-co - pa ta–a   syn-co - pa syn-co - pa   syn-co - pa ta–a

2

ta   ta   ta   ta   ti ti ti ti ti ti ti ti   ti ti ka ti ti ti ti ka ti ti   ta   ta   ta–a

Evaluation

Demonstrate how well you have learned the skills and concepts featured in the lesson "Little David, Play On Your Harp" by completing the following:

- As a duet or in a small group, perform measures 1–19 to show your understanding of imitation while singing.

- Look in your music at measures 4 and 12. Which measure is an example of syncopation and which is an example of non-syncopation? Support your answer. Find other examples of each in your music.

This arrangement for
Priscilla Gaston and the Crockett Sixth Grade Choir

Little David, Play On Your Harp

For 2-Part and Piano

Arranged by
EMILY CROCKER

African American Spiritual

Lit-tle Da-vid

Lit-tle Da-vid

play on your harp, hal - le - lu, hal - le - lu, Lit-tle Da-vid play on your harp, hal - le -

play on your harp, hal - le - lu, hal - le - lu, Lit-tle Da-vid play on your harp, hal - le -

lu! Lit-tle Da-vid, Lit-tle Da-vid play on your harp play on your harp,

lu! Lit-tle Da-vid play on your harp, hal - le - lu, hal - le - lu, Lit-tle Da-vid

Pokare Kare Ana

Composer: Paware Tomoana, arranged by Mark O'Leary
Text: Paware Tomoana
Voicing: 2-Part

VOCABULARY

diction

syllabic stress

skipwise motion

Focus

- Perform music with correct diction and syllabic stress.
- Understand music in relation to history and culture.

SPOTLIGHT

To learn more about diction, see page 33.

Getting Started

In any language, vocal music can be used to express emotions or to tell a story. Therefore, when singing, it is important to convey the meaning of the text through your body language and facial expression. It is also important to use proper **diction** (*the pronunciation of words while singing*) and correct syllabic stress so that you can be clearly understood.

Syllabic stress is *the stressing of one syllable over another*. For example, in the word *music*, you would stress the first syllable more than the second. You would sing, "MU-sic," rather than "mu-SIC." Discuss where you would place the syllabic stress on the words *father, telephone,* and *America*.

◆ History and Culture

"Pokare Kare Ana" is a love song from New Zealand. Sung in the Maori language, it tells the story of Princess Hinemoa and Tutaneki, a warrior who lived on an island nine miles from shore. Hinemoa's father would not allow the couple to see each other. Every night Tutaneki would serenade Hinemoa by playing his flute, and the sound would travel across the water to her. One night, Hinemoa decided to swim to her warrior's island. Soon after, Hinemoa and Tutaneki were married, and many tribes developed from the descendants of this couple.

Links to Learning

◆ Vocal

Skipwise motion means *to skip two or more notes away from a given note on the staff.*
Read and perform the following example to develop accurate intonation while
singing in skipwise motion.

do   sol   do   sol   do   mi   do   sol   mi   do

◆ Theory

Perform the following example to practice singing the opening phrase of "Pokare
Kare Ana." Notice the skipwise motion.

loo   loo loo loo loo   loo   loo,____   loo   loo loo loo loo   loo   loo,__

____ loo loo loo loo loo loo   loo   loo,_____   loo   loo loo loo loo   loo

◆ Artistic Expression

To develop artistry in singing through proper diction and syllabic stress, chant
and sing the following example. Place a slight stress on the syllables that are printed
in capital letters.

Po - KA-re KA-re   A   -   na,_____   nga WAI o Ro-to-RU - a,____

__ WHI-ti A - tu KO-e HI   -   ne,_____   MA - RI-no A - na   E.

Evaluation

Demonstrate how well you have learned the skills and concepts featured in the
lesson "Pokare Kare Ana" by completing the following:

- Apply your knowledge of syllabic stress by singing the second verse of
  "Pokare Kare Ana" (measures 9–16) with correct diction and syllabic stress.

- Describe the cultural background of this piece in your own words.

Pokare Kare Ana

For 2-Part and Piano or Guitar* with Optional Flutes**

Arranged by
MARK O'LEARY

Words and Music by
PAWARE TOMOANA

* Although originally scored for guitar, piano may be used. Pianist should imitate smooth, guitar-like playing. Guitar should use chord symbols above piano and rhythms indicated in piano.

**Flute part found on page 196.

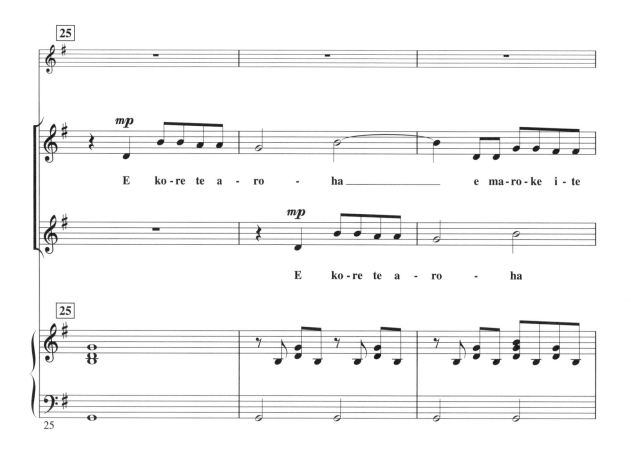

E ko-re te a-ro - ha _____ e ma-ro-ke i - te

E ko-re te a-ro - ha

ra. _____ Ma - ku - ku to - nu _____

e ma-ro-ke i - te ra. _____ Ma - ku - ku

Am

D

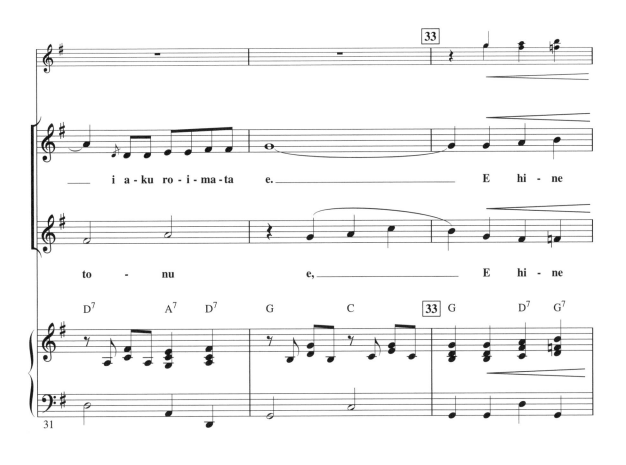

i a-ku ro-i-ma-ta e. _____ E hi - ne

to - nu e, _____ E hi - ne

e, _____ Ho - ki mai ra, _____ Ka ma-te a -

e, _____ Ho - ki mai ra, _____ Ka ma-te a -

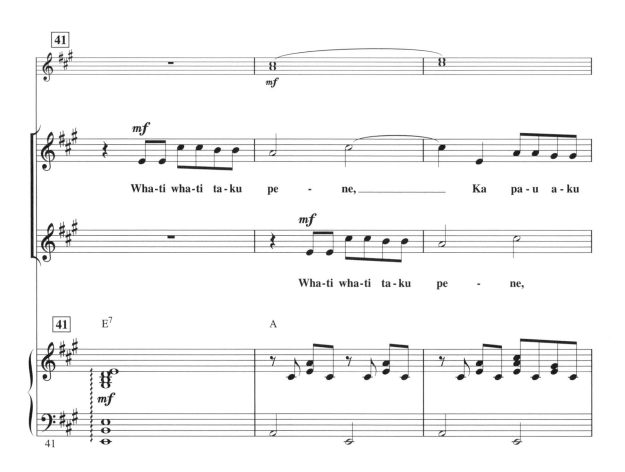

e, _____ Ho - ki mai ra. _____ Ka ma - te a -

e, _____ Ho - ki mai ra. _____ Ka ma - te a -

hau i - te a - ro - ha e, _____ E hi - ne

hau i - te a - ro - ha e, _____ E hi - ne

e,_____ Ho - ki mai ra,_____ Ka ma - te a -

e,_____ Ho - ki mai ra,_____ Ka ma - te a -

D   A

hau i - te a - ro - ha e._____

hau i - te a - ro - ha e._____

E   E⁷ B⁷ E⁷   A   D   A

Pokare Kare Ana

For 2-Part and Piano or Guitar with Optional Flutes

FLUTE 1, 2

Words and Music by PAWARE TOMOANA
Arranged by MARK O'LEARY

Río, Río

Composer: Chilean Folk Song, arranged by Audrey Snyder
Text: Traditional Spanish
Voicing: 2-Part

VOCABULARY

$\frac{6}{8}$ meter

tied notes

unison

Focus

- Recognize the difference between unison and part-singing.
- Relate other subjects to music.
- Develop criteria for evaluating music.

SPOTLIGHT

To learn more about pitch matching, see page 83.

Getting Started

Why are people so fascinated by rivers? Through the course of time, artists have been inspired to write songs, poems, and books about rivers. Often, human feelings and emotions are used to describe them. Country singer Garth Brooks sings, "You know a dream is like a river, ever changing as it flows." The famous poet Solaz wrote, "I am a fathomless river; untold riches and treasures are hidden in my deeps." As you learn "Río, Río," you will notice the human characteristics given to the river.

◆ History and Culture

The people of Chile have a tradition of living life with enthusiasm. This lifestyle is reflected in vibrant music, flavorful food, and festive celebrations. Rivers play an important part in the lives of the Chilean people. These rivers are tourist attractions as well as sources of enjoyment and productivity.

Written in Spanish, "Río, Río" (translated "River, River") is a folk song of unknown origin. However, a historic tale of a Chilean military leader and his wife parallels its text. The military leader went off to war and his wife longed for his return. Read the words found in "Río, Río." Do you think this story fits the text?

Links to Learning

◆ **Vocal**

Perform the following example to practice singing some of the melodic patterns found in "Río, Río."

Rí - o,   rí - o,   rí - o,   rí - o.

◆ **Theory**

Read and perform the following example to practice rhythmic patterns in $\frac{6}{8}$ **meter**, *a time signature in which there are six beats to a measure and the dotted quarter note receives the beat.* Observe the **tied notes** (*two notes of the same pitch that are joined together to form one longer note*) in the example.

ta   ti ti ti ti   ta   ti ti ti ti   ta   ta   ti ti   ti ti ti tam

Although this arrangement of "Río, Río" is written in two parts, there are sections throughout where both parts sing in **unison** (*all parts sing the same notes at the same time*). Look at the music and locate the parts that are sung in unison.

◆ **Artistic Expression**

Poets have often written about rivers. Find a poem about a river to read to the class. As a class, discuss the various characteristics given to rivers in each poem.

Evaluation

Demonstrate how well you have learned the skills and concepts featured in the lesson "Río, Río" by completing the following:

- Sing measures 14–29 with another student, one on each part. Write a short self-evaluation of your performance by answering the following questions:
  - When singing in unison, did your voices match pitch?
  - When singing in harmony, could both parts be heard?
  - Could the melody line be heard over the harmony line?
  - Was the rhythm performed correctly?

  Collect feedback from several students by asking them the same questions. Compare your answers. Share what you have learned.

- As a class, decide which poems should be read at a performance of "Río, Río."

Río, Río
(River, River)

For 2-Part and Piano

Arranged by
AUDREY SNYDER

Chilean Folk Song

Sourwood Mountain

Composer: American Folk Song, arranged by Shirley W. McRae
Text: Traditional
Voicing: 3-Part Treble

VOCABULARY

strophic

strophe

refrain

$\frac{2}{4}$ meter

Focus

- Identify musical form.

- Sing with expression and technical accuracy.

- Read rhythmic patterns with sixteenth notes.

 **SKILL BUILDERS**

To learn more about $\frac{2}{4}$ *meter, see* Beginning Sight-Singing, *page 59.*

Getting Started

Like many folk songs, "Sourwood Mountain" is **strophic**, in that *the melody repeats while the words change from verse to verse*. For example, the melody of the first **strophe**, or *verse*, is the same as both the second and third strophes. Although the melody repeats, the rhythms vary slightly to accommodate the words in each strophe. What other strophic folk songs do you know?

Another feature common to folk music is the **refrain,** *a repeated section at the end of each phrase*. In "Sourwood Mountain," the refrain is made up of the nonsense syllables, "hi-o, hi-o, diddle-i-day."

◆ History and Culture

Though it is likely that the song "Sourwood Mountain" arrived with the eighteenth-century pioneers from the British Isles, its history in the United States lies in the southern Appalachian Mountains. The Appalachians form the second-largest mountain range in North America. They extend from Quebec, Canada, to Alabama. Southern Appalachia includes parts of West Virginia, Virginia, Kentucky, Tennessee, North and South Carolina, Georgia, and Alabama. This area was originally inhabited by Native Americans, including the Cherokee.

Links to Learning

◆ **Vocal**

Read and perform the following example to practice three-part singing.

◆ **Theory**

$\frac{2}{4}$ **meter** is *a time signature in which there are two beats per measure and the quarter note receives the beat.* Read and perform the following examples to practice reading rhythmic patterns with sixteenth notes in $\frac{2}{4}$ meter.

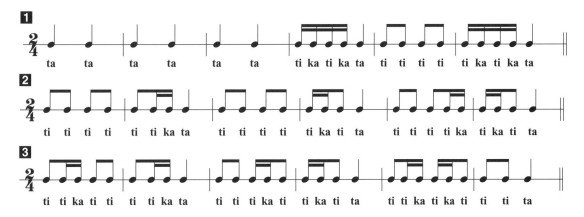

Evaluation

Demonstrate how well you have learned the skills and concepts featured in the lesson "Sourwood Mountain" by completing the following:

- Find the fourth and fifth strophe in the music to show that you understand strophic form.

- Sing one strophe alone to demonstrate accurate intonation, precise rhythm, and clear diction.

- Alone or with others, read and clap the rhythmic patterns found in the Theory section above. Evaluate how well you did.

This arrangement dedicated to the
1996 North Carolina Summer Institute in Choral Art
Elementary Choir, Henry Leck, Director

Sourwood Mountain

For 3-Part Treble and Piano with Optional Flute**

Arranged by
SHIRLEY W. McRAE

American Folk Song

1. Chick - ens crow-in' on Sour - wood Moun-tain, Hi - o, hi - o, did-dle-i - day,

Get your dog and we'll go hunt - in', Hi - o, hi - o, did-dle-i - day.

* Pronounced dih-duhl-eye-day.
** Flute part found on page 217.

Hi - o, hi - o, did-dle-i - day.

3. My true love is blue-eyed Dai-sy, Hi - o, hi - o, did-dle-i - day,

Hi, hi, did-dle-i - day,

Hi, hi, did-dle-i - day,

4. My true love is in the hol - ler, Hi - o, hi - o,

did-dle - i - day, He won't come and I won't fol - ler,

Hi - o, hi - o, did-dle-i - day.

Sourwood Mountain

FLUTE

Southern Folk Song
Arranged by SHIRLEY W. McRAE

Tinga Layo

Composer: West Indies Folk Song, arranged by Cristi Cary Miller
Text: Traditional
Voicing: 3-Part Mixed

VOCABULARY

calypso

chord

harmony

dynamics

Focus

- Sing in three-part harmony.
- Identify and perform standard notation for dynamics.
- Perform music that represents calypso of the West Indies.

 SPOTLIGHT

To learn more about the changing voice, see page 231.

Getting Started

Perhaps you know the song "Tinga Layo." It is a popular children's folk song from the Caribbean and a perfect example of calypso music. **Calypso** is *a style of music that comes from the West Indies and features syncopated rhythms and comical lyrics.* In this calypso song, you will sing about a donkey that walks, talks, and eats with a fork and spoon!

◆ History and Culture

The Caribbean region (West Indies) encompasses a chain of islands stretching over 2,000 miles from the southern coast of Florida to the northern coast of Venezuela, South America. Historically, the West Indies are known for producing sugar cane, coconuts, and bananas. Today some of these islands, which include Barbados, Puerto Rico, and the Virgin Islands, are popular tourist destinations. They provide tropical paradises and feature exciting music, lush vegetation, beautiful beaches, and crystal-clear seas.

Links to Learning

◆ Vocal

When *three or more notes are sung together*, a **chord** is formed and harmony is created. **Harmony** occurs *when two or more different notes or melodies are sung at the same time*. Practice the following chords to develop the skill of singing in harmony.

◆ Theory

Read and perform the following examples to practice reading rhythmic patterns with syncopation.

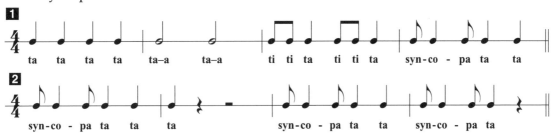

◆ Artistic Expression

One way to add expression to a musical performance is through the use of **dynamics**, or *symbols that indicate to a musician how loud or soft to sing or play*. In the Vocal examples above, sing example 1 *mf*, or *mezzo forte* (medium loud); sing example 2 *mp*, or *mezzo piano* (medium soft); and sing example 3 *f*, or *forte* (loud).

Evaluation

Demonstrate how well you have learned the skills featured in the lesson "Tinga Layo" by completing the following:

- In a trio with one singer on each part, perform measures 4–12 of "Tinga Layo." How well were you able to sing in three-part harmony?

- Sing measures 5–24. As you perform, adjust your dynamic levels as marked at measures 5–6 (*mp*), measures 12–13 (*f*), measures 16–17 (*mf*), and measures 20–21 (*mp*).

Tinga Layo

For 3-Part Mixed and Piano with Optional Percussion**

Arranged by
CRISTI CARY MILLER

West Indies Folk Song

*Pronounced "ting-gah lay-oh."

**Percussion part found on pages 229 and 230.

Tinga Layo

PERCUSSION
(Cowbell, Maracas, Conga Drums)

West Indies Folk Song
Arranged by
CRISTI CARY MILLER

SPOTLIGHT

Changing Voice

As we grow in size and maturity, we don't always grow at the same rate. Just look around your school or neighborhood. Some thirteen-year-olds tower over others, while some are quite small.

As the voice matures, it changes in both pitch and **timbre** *(tone quality)*. Just like growing in stature, this process is not the same for every person. One person's voice might drop an octave almost overnight, while another person's might not seem to have changed at all.

The Male Voice

As a young male singer, you will face several challenges as your voice matures. Certain pitches that were once easy to sing suddenly may be out of your vocal range. While every voice change is unique, many male singers progress through several identifiable stages:

1. The voice is a treble voice with no obvious signs of changing.

2. The upper range sounds slightly breathy or hoarse.

3. The singer is able to sing lower pitches than before. Higher pitches continue to sound breathy. The speaking and singing voices are noticeably lower. There is an obvious "break" around middle C.

4. The voice "settles" into **Bass** *(the lowest-sounding male voice)* or "rises" to **Tenor** *(the highest-sounding male voice)*. Higher pitches can now be sung in **falsetto,** *a register in the male voice that extends far above the natural high voice.*

With practice and attention to the principles of good singing, you can get through this transition without too much difficulty.

The Female Voice

As a young female singer, you will not face the same challenges that young male singers face. However, your voice will go through changes, too.

Between the ages of eleven and sixteen, you might notice breathiness in your vocal tone, difficulty in moving between your chest voice and head voice, and a general lack of vocal resonance.

By using the good vocal techniques of posture, breath and vowel formation, you can establish all the qualities necessary for success. You should use your full vocal range and gain experience in singing both **Alto** *(the lowest-sounding female voice)* and **Soprano** *(the highest-sounding female voice),* since your actual voice category may not be evident until you reach your middle-to-late teens.

Unity

Composer: Glorraine B. Moone and Rev. Freddie Washington, arranged by Daniel M. Cason II
Text: Psalm 133:1, with additional text by Glorraine B. Moone
Voicing: SSA

VOCABULARY

gospel music

rote

chest voice

Focus

- Extend your vocal range.

- Read and perform rhythmic patterns with sixteenth notes.

- Perform music in the gospel style.

 **SKILL BUILDERS**

To learn more about dotted eighth and sixteenth note combinations, see Beginning Sight-Singing, *page 92.*

Getting Started

Unity can be defined as "many standing together as one." Throughout history, people have demonstrated unity through both good and bad times. On a more personal basis, friends often stand together united as one. By singing "Unity," you can express the importance of unity, peace, and friendship in your life.

◆ History and Culture

Gospel music is *religious music that originated in the African American churches of the South.* During the early 1900s, the gospel sound spread to other parts of the United States. As many African Americans migrated to the North and the West, they took with them their songs of praise—their gospel music.

Originally, gospel music was taught by **rote,** or *taught by singing a song over and over again.* Today, many printed arrangements exist, making gospel music accessible to more people. In this arrangement, the composer draws from the biblical text, "Behold how good and how pleasant it is for brethren to dwell together in unity," and combines it with her own text. The result is an expressive song that calls for unity among all people.

On page 168 in this book, you will find the lesson to "Hine ma tov," a Hebrew folk song. It is based on the same text as "Unity." Listen to both songs and discuss the ways in which two different cultures have chosen to express a similar theme of unity and peace.

Links to Learning

◆ Vocal

The melody in "Unity" begins in the **chest voice,** or *the lower part of your vocal range.* Perform the following example to gently develop and expand your chest voice. Keep the "ah" vowel relaxed and not forced.

mee___ ah_____   mee___ ah_____ (etc.)

◆ Theory

Perform the following sixteenth-note patterns used in "Unity." Form two groups. At the same time, one group pats the steady quarter notes while the other group taps the rhythm. Keep the tempo slow and relaxed to reflect the gospel style. Switch roles.

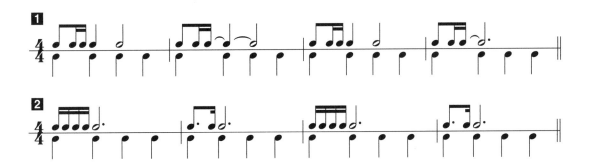

Evaluation

Demonstrate how well you have learned the skills and concepts featured in lesson "Unity" by completing the following:

- Sing the Vocal example above. With the help of your teacher, find the lowest note in your own vocal range that can be sung relaxed, sustained, and with accurate pitch.

- Perform measures 12–19 of "Unity" in small groups to show the correct usage of the sixteenth-note rhythmic patterns.

- African American history and culture are the foundation for many important musical styles, including spirituals, jazz, gospel, rap, and rhythm and blues. Make a chart of the songs that you know for each style of music listed above. Sing one of the songs and demonstrate the style for your friends.

Unity

For SSA and Piano

Arranged and Scored by
DANIEL M. CASON II

Words from Psalm 133:1
Additional text by GLORRAINE B. MOONE
Music by GLORRAINE B. MOONE
and REV. FREDDIE WASHINGTON

Yonder Come Day

Composer: Georgia Sea Islands Spiritual, arranged by Judith Cook Tucker
Text: Traditional, with additional words by Judith Cook Tucker
Voicing: 3-Part, Any Combination

VOCABULARY

body percussion

a cappella

breath support

patsch

 SPOTLIGHT

To learn more about breath management, see page 21.

Focus

- Sing with good breath support.

- Evaluate the quality and effectiveness of performances.

- Perform music from the Georgia Sea Islands.

Getting Started

What kind of games do you enjoy playing? What kind of games do you think children played many years ago before there was electricity? Possibly, the children played "Kick the Can" or "Hide and Seek." At other times, they might have played singing games. Often, while singing, they would add **body percussion** by *clapping, stepping, or slapping their thighs.* Make a game of "Yonder Come Day" by adding the suggested body percussion movements, or make up your own!

◆ History and Culture

"Yonder Come Day" comes from the Georgia Sea Islands, which are located along the outer banks of Georgia. From the late 1700s until the Civil War, slaves worked on the plantations found on these islands. Geographically, the slaves were cut off from the mainland, as connecting bridges were not built until many years later. As a result, the rich African culture, songs, and games were preserved. The native people developed their own language, a mixture of English and African dialect known as *Gullah.* Their songs were traditionally sung **a cappella,** or *without instruments.* In place of instruments, a common practice was the use of body percussion to accompany these songs.

Links to Learning

◆ **Vocal**

Breath support, or *a constant airflow,* is necessary to produce sound for singing. Perform the following exercise to help develop this skill.

> Breathe in air through an imaginary straw. Exhale on a "hiss." First inhale and exhale over 6 counts, then 10 counts, then 12.

For more practice, place the palm of one hand three or four inches from your mouth. As you sing the following example, you should feel a steady stream of warm air on your palm. Then take your hand away, but continue to sing in the manner above.

Yon - der,___ yon - der,___ yon - der,___ yon - der.___

◆ **Artistic Expression**

To develop artistry through movement, perform the opening phrase of "Yonder Come Day" (measures 3–10) while doing the body percussion movements indicated below. The word **patsch** means *to slap your hands on your thighs.*

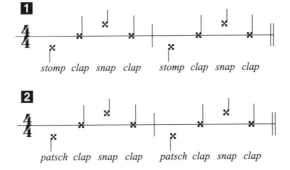

Evaluation

Demonstrate how well you have learned the skills and concepts featured in the lesson "Yonder Come Day" by completing the following:

- To show that you can sing with appropriate breath support, sing measures 3–10, taking a breath only at the end of measure 6.

- With the assistance of your teacher, videotape your class performing "Yonder Come Day." View the video and evaluate how well you were able to use the body percussion movements during your performance.

Yonder Come Day

For 3-Part, Any Combination, a cappella

Arranged by
JUDITH COOK TUCKER

Based on the traditional
Georgia Sea Islands Spiritual
Additional words and music by
JUDITH COOK TUCKER

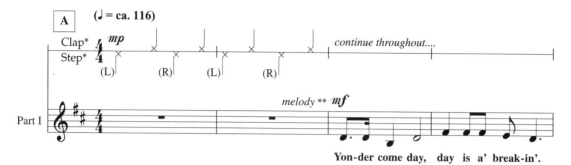

*Begin with step/clap for two measures.
**Sing melody once or twice through in unison before layering in parts.

*At D.S., repeat Section C as many times as desired. On the last repeat, observe ritard and hold last note.

sun - rise, oh yon - der, sun -

Yon - der come day, oh, my___ soul.___ Yon - der come day,

yon - der,___ yon - der.___ Yon - der,___

21

rise. Sun is a' ri - sin' in my soul.___

day is a' break-in'. Sun is a' ris - in' in my soul.___

yon - der,___ Sun is a' ris - in' in my___ soul.___ (Oh, well 'a)

24

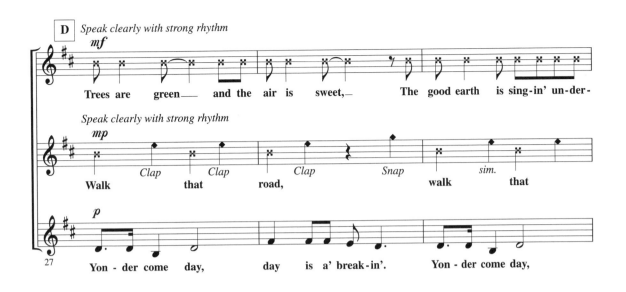

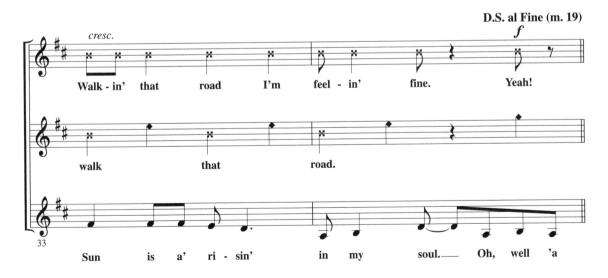

Glossary

CHORAL MUSIC TERMS

2/2 meter   A time signature in which there are two beats per measure and the half note receives the beat.

2/4 meter   A time signature in which there are two beats per measure and the quarter note receives the beat.

3/2 meter   A time signature in which there are three beats per measure and the half note receives the beat.

3/4 meter   A time signature in which there are three beats per measure and the quarter note receives the beat.

3/8 meter   A time signature in which there is one group of three eighth notes per measure and the dotted quarter note receives the beat. When the tempo is very slow, this meter can be counted as having three beats per measure, with the eighth note receiving the beat.

4/4 meter   A time signature in which there are four beats per measure and the quarter note receives the beat.

5/8 meter   A time signature in which there are five beats per measure and the eighth note receives the beat.

6/4 meter   A time signature in which there are two groups of three quarter notes per measure and the dotted half note receives the beat. When the tempo is very slow, this meter can be counted as having six beats per measure, with the quarter note receiving the beat.

6/8 meter   A time signature in which there are two groups of three eighth notes per measure and the dotted quarter note receives the beat. When the tempo is very slow, this meter can be counted as having six beats per measure, with the eighth note receiving the beat.

9/8 meter   A time signature in which there are three groups of three eighth notes per measure and the dotted quarter note receives the beat. When the tempo is very slow, this meter can be counted as having nine beats per measure, with the eighth note receiving the beat.

12/8 meter   A time signature in which there are four groups of three eighth notes per measure and the dotted quarter note receives the beat.

A

a cappella *(ah-kah-PEH-lah)* [It.] A style of singing without instrumental accompaniment.

a tempo *(ah TEM-poh)* [It.] A tempo marking which indicates to return to the original tempo of a piece or section of music.

ABA form   A form in which an opening section (A) is followed by a contrasting section (B), which leads to the repetition of the opening section (A).

accelerando *(accel.) (ah-chel-leh-RAHN-doh)* [It.] A tempo marking that indicates to gradually get faster.

accent   A symbol placed above or below a given note to indicate that the note should receive extra emphasis or stress. ($\overset{>}{\bullet}$)

accidental   Any sharp, flat or natural that is not included in the key signature of a piece of music.

adagio *(ah-DAH-jee-oh)* [It.] Slow tempo, but not as slow as *largo*.

ad libitum *(ad. lib.)* [Lt.] An indication that the performer may vary the tempo or add or delete a vocal or instrumental part.

Aeolian scale *(ay-OH-lee-an)* [Gk.] A modal scale that starts and ends on *la*. It is made up of the same arrangement of whole and half steps as a natural minor scale.

al fine *(ahl FEE-neh)* [It.] To the end.

aleatory music *(AY-lee-uh-toh-ree)* A type of music in which certain aspects are performed randomly. Also known as chance music.

alla breve   Indicates cut time; a duple meter in which there are two beats per measure, and half note receives the beat. *See* cut time.

allargando (allarg.) (ahl-ahr-GAHN-doh) [It.] To broaden, become slower.

allegro (ah-LEH-groh) [It.] Brisk tempo; faster than *moderato*, slower than *vivace*.

allegro non troppo (ah-LEH-groh nohn TROH-poh) [It.] A tempo marking that indicates not too fast. Not as fast as *allegro*.

altered pitch Another name for an accidental.

alto (AL-toh) The lowest-sounding female voice.

andante (ahn-DAHN- teh) [It.] Moderately slow; a walking tempo.

andante con moto (ahn-DAHN- teh kohn MOH-toh) [It.] A slightly faster tempo, "with motion."

animato Quickly, lively; "animated."

anthem A choral composition in English using a sacred text.

arpeggio (ahr-PEH-jee-oh) [It.] A chord in which the pitches are sounded successively, usually from lowest to highest; in broken style.

arrangement A piece of music in which a composer takes an existing melody and adds extra features or changes the melody in some way.

arranger A composer who takes an original or existing melody and adds extra features or changes the melody in some way.

art song A musical setting of a poem.

articulation The amount of separation or connection between notes.

articulators The lips, teeth, tongue and other parts of the mouth and throat that are used to produce vocal sound.

avocational Not related to a job or career.

barbershop A style of *a cappella* singing in which three parts harmonize with the melody. The lead sings the melody while the tenor harmonizes above and the baritone and bass harmonize below.

barcarole A Venetian boat song.

baritone The male voice between tenor and bass.

barline A vertical line placed on the musical staff that groups notes and rests together.

Baroque period (bah-ROHK) [Fr.] The historical period in Western civilization from 1600 to 1750.

bass The lowest-sounding male voice.

bass clef A clef that generally indicates notes that sound lower than middle C.

basso continuo (BAH-soh cun-TIN-you-oh) [It.] A continually moving bass line, common in music from the Baroque period.

beat The steady pulse of music.

bebop style Popular in jazz, music that features notes that are light, lively and played quickly. Often the melodic lines are complex and follow unpredictable patterns.

blues scale An altered major scale that uses flatted or lowered third, fifth and seventh notes: *ma* (lowered from *mi*), *se* (lowered from *sol*) and *te* (lowered from *ti*).

blues style An original African American art form that developed in the early twentieth century in the Mississippi Delta region of the South. The lyrics often express feelings of frustration, hardship or longing. It often contains elements such as call and response, the blues scale and swing.

body percussion The use of one's body to make a percussive sound, such as clapping, snapping or stepping.

breath mark A symbol in vocal music used to indicate where a singer should take a breath. (')

breath support A constant airflow necessary to produce sound for singing.

cadence A melodic or harmonic structure that marks the end of a phrase or the completion of a song.

call and response A derivative of the field hollers used by slaves as they worked. A leader or group sings a phrase (call) followed by a response of the same phrase by another group.

calypso A style of music that originated in the West Indies and which features syncopated rhythms and comical lyrics.

canon A musical form in which one part sings a melody, and the other parts sing the same melody, but enter at different times. Canons are sometimes called rounds.

cantabile *(con-TAH-bee-leh)* [It.] In a lyrical, singing style.

cantata *(con-TAH-tah)* [It.] A large-scale musical piece made up of several movements for singers and instrumentalists. Johann Sebastian Bach was a prominent composer of cantatas.

cantor *(CAN-tor)* A person who sings and/or teaches music in a temple or synagogue.

canzona [It.] A rhythmic instrumental composition that is light and fast-moving.

chamber music Music performed by a small instrumental ensemble, generally with one instrument per part. The string quartet is a popular form of chamber music, consisting of two violins, a viola and a cello. Chamber music was popular during the Classical period.

chantey *See* sea chantey.

chanteyman A soloist who improvised and led the singing of sea chanteys.

chest voice The lower part of the singer's vocal range.

chorale *(kuh-RAL)* [Gr.] Congregational song or hymn of the German Protestant Church.

chord The combination of three or more notes played or sung together at the same time.

chromatic scale *(kroh-MAT-tick)* [Gk.] A scale that consists of all half steps and uses all twelve pitches in an octave.

Classical period The historical period in Western civilization from 1750 to 1820.

clef The symbol at the beginning of a staff that indicates which lines and spaces represent which notes.

coda A special ending to a song. A concluding section of a composition. (⊕)

common time Another name for 4/4 meter. Also known as common meter. (𝄴)

composer A person who takes a musical thought and writes it out in musical notation to share it with others.

compound meter Any meter in which the dotted quarter note receives the beat, and the division of the beat is based on three eighth notes. 6/8, 9/8 and 12/8 are examples of compound meter.

con moto *(kohn MOH-toh)* [It.] With motion.

concert etiquette A term used to describe what is appropriate behavior in formal or informal musical performances.

concerto *(cun-CHAIR-toh)* [Fr., It.] A composition for a solo instrument and orchestra.

concerto grosso *(cun-CHAIR-toh GROH-soh)* [Fr., It.] A multimovement Baroque piece for a group of soloists and an orchestra.

conductor A person who uses hand and arm gestures to interpret the expressive elements of music for singers and instrumentalists.

conductus A thirteenth-century song for two, three or four voices.

consonance Harmonies in chords or music that are pleasing to the ear.

Contemporary period The historical period from 1900 to the present.

countermelody A separate melodic line that supports and/or contrasts the melody of a piece of music.

counterpoint The combination of two or more melodic lines. The parts move independently while harmony is created. Johann Sebastian Bach is considered by many to be one of the greatest composers of contrapuntal music.

contrary motion A technique in which two melodic lines move in opposite directions.

crescendo *(creh-SHEN-doh)* [It.] A dynamic marking that indicates to gradually sing or play louder.

cut time Another name for 2/2 meter. (¢)

D
---

da capo *(D.C.)* *(dah KAH-poh)* [It.] Go back to the beginning and repeat; *see* dal segno *and* al fine.

dal segno *(D.S.)* *(dahl SAYN-yah)* [It.] Go back to the sign and repeat.

D. C. al Fine *(FEE-nay)* [It.] A term that indicates to go back to the beginning and repeat. The term *al fine* indicates to sing to the end, or *fine*.

decrescendo *(DAY-creh-shen-doh)* [It.] A dynamic marking that indicates to gradually sing or play softer.

descant A special part in a piece of music that is usually sung higher than the melody or other parts of the song.

diatonic scale *(die-uh-TAH-nick)* A scale that uses no altered pitches or accidentals. Both the major scale and the natural minor scale are examples of a diatonic scale.

diction The pronunciation of words while singing.

diminished chord A minor chord in which the top note is lowered one half step from *mi* to *me*.

diminuendo *(dim.)* *(duh-min-yoo-WEN-doh)* [It.] Gradually getting softer; *see* decrescendo.

diphthong A combination of two vowel sounds.

dissonance A combination of pitches or tones that clash.

dolce *(DOHL-chay)* [It.] Sweetly.

dominant chord A chord built on the fifth note of a scale. In a major scale, this chord uses the notes *sol, ti* and *re*, and it may be called the **V** ("five") chord, since it is based on the fifth note of the major scale, or *sol*. In a minor scale, this chord uses the notes *mi, sol* and *ti* (or *mi, si* and *ti*), and it may be called the **v** or **V** ("five") chord, since it is based on the fifth note of the minor scale, or *mi*.

Dorian scale *(DOOR-ee-an)* [Gk.] A modal scale that starts and ends on *re*.

dot A symbol that increases the length of a given note by half its value. It is placed to the right of the note.

dotted half note A note that represents three beats of sound when the quarter note receives the beat.

double barline A set of two barlines that indicate the end of a piece or section of music.

D. S. al coda *(dahl SAYN-yoh ahl KOH-dah)* [It.] Repeat from the symbol (％) and skip to the coda when you see the sign. (⊕)

duet A group of two singers or instrumentalists.

dynamics Symbols in music that indicate how loud or soft to sing or play.

E
---

eighth note A note that represents one half beat of sound when the quarter note receives the beat. Two eighth notes equal one beat of sound when the quarter note receives the beat.

eighth rest A rest that represents one half beat of silence when the quarter note receives the beat. Two eighth rests equal one beat of silence when the quarter note receives the beat.

expressive singing To sing with feeling.

F

falsetto [It.] The register in the male voice that extends far above the natural voice. The light upper range.

fermata *(fur-MAH-tah)* [It.] A symbol that indicates to hold a note or rest for longer than its given value. (⌢)

fine *(fee-NAY)* [It.] A term used to indicate the end of a piece of music.

flat A symbol that lowers the pitch of a given note by one half step.(♭)

folk music Music that passed down from generation to generation through oral tradition. Traditional music that reflects a place, event or a national feeling.

folk song A song passed down from generation to generation through oral tradition. A song that reflects a place, event or a national feeling.

form The structure or design of a musical composition.

forte *(FOR-tay)* [It.] A dynamic that indicates to sing or play loud. (*f*)

fortissimo *(for-TEE-see-moh)* [It.] A dynamic that indicates to sing or play very loud. (*ff*)

fugue *(FYOOG)* A musical form in which the same melody is performed by different instruments or voices entering at different times, thus adding layers of sound.

fusion Music that is developed by the act of combining various types and cultural influences of music into a new style.

G

gospel music Religious music that originated in the African American churches of the South. This music can be characterized by improvisation, syncopation and repetition.

grand staff A staff that is created when two staves are joined together.

grandioso [It.] Stately, majestic.

grave *(GRAH-veh)* [It.] Slow, solemn.

grazioso *(grah-tsee-OH-soh)* [It.] Graceful.

Gregorian chant A single, unaccompanied melodic line sung by male voices. Featuring a sacred text and used in the church, this style of music was developed in the Medieval period.

H

half note A note that represents two beats of sound when the quarter note receives the beat. ♩

half rest A rest that represents two beats of silence when the quarter note receives the beat. ▬

half step The smallest distance (interval) between two notes on a keyboard; the chromatic scale is composed entirely of half steps.

harmonic minor scale A minor scale that uses a raised seventh note, *si* (raised from *sol*).

harmonics Small whistle-like tones, or overtones, that are sometimes produced over a sustained pitch.

harmony A musical sound that is formed when two or more different pitches are played or sung at the same time.

head voice The higher part of the singer's vocal range.

homophonic *(hah-muh-FAH-nik)* [Gk.] A texture where all parts sing similar rhythm in unison or harmony.

homophony *(haw-MAW-faw-nee)* [Gk.] A type of music in which there are two or more parts with similar or identical rhythms being sung or played at the same time. Also, music in which melodic interest is concentrated in one voice part and may have subordinate accompaniment.

hushed A style marking indicating a soft, whispered tone.

imitation The act of one part copying what another part has already played or sung.

improvisation The art of singing or playing music, making it up as you go, or composing and performing a melody at the same time.

International Phonetic Alphabet (IPA) A phonetic alphabet that provides a notational standard for all languages. Developed in Paris, France in 1886.

interval The distance between two notes.

intonation The accuracy of pitch, in-tune singing.

Ionian scale (*eye-OWN-ee-an*) [Gk.] A modal scale that starts and ends on *do*. It is made up of the same arrangement of whole and half steps as a major scale.

jazz An original American style of music that features swing rhythms, syncopation and improvisation.

jongleur [Fr.] An entertainer who traveled from town to town during medieval times, often telling stories and singing songs.

key Determined by a song's or scale's home tone, or keynote.

key signature A symbol or set of symbols that determines the key of a piece of music.

ledger lines Short lines that appear above, between treble and bass clefs, or below the bass clef, used to expand the notation.

legato (*leh-GAH-toh*) [It.] A connected and sustained style of singing and playing.

lento (*LEN-toh*) [It.] Slow; a little faster than *largo*, a little slower than *adagio*.

lied (*leet*) [Ger.] A song in the German language, generally with a secular text.

liturgical text A text that has been written for the purpose of worship in a church setting.

lute An early form of the guitar.

Lydian scale (*LIH-dee-an*) [Gk.] A modal scale that starts and ends on *fa*.

lyrics The words of a song.

madrigal A poem that has been set to music in the language of the composer. Featuring several imitative parts, it usually has a secular text and is generally sung *a cappella*.

maestoso (*mah-eh-STOH-soh*) [It.] Perform majestically.

major chord A chord that can be based on the *do, mi,* and *sol* of a major scale.

major scale A scale that has *do* as its home tone, or keynote. It is made up of a specific arrangement of whole steps and half steps in the following order: W + W + H + W + W + W + H.

major tonality A song that is based on a major scale with *do* as its keynote, or home tone.

mangulina A traditional dance from the Dominican Republic.

marcato (*mar-CAH-toh*) [It.] A stressed and accented style of singing and playing.

mass   A religious service of prayers and ceremonies originating in the Roman Catholic Church consisting of spoken and sung sections. It consists of several sections divided into two groups: proper (text changes for every day) and ordinary (text stays the same in every mass). Between the years 1400 and 1600, the mass assumed its present form consisting of the Kyrie, Gloria, Credo, Sanctus and Agnus Dei. It may include chants, hymns and psalms as well. The mass also developed into large musical works for chorus, soloists and even orchestra.

measure   The space between two barlines.

Medieval period   The historical period in Western civilization also known as the Middle Ages (400–1430).

medley   A collection of songs musically linked together.

melisma *(muh-LIZ-mah)* [Gk.] A group of notes sung to a single syllable or word.

melismatic singing *(muh-liz-MAT-ik)* [Gk.] A style of text setting in which one syllable is sung over many notes.

melodic contour   The overall shape of the melody.

melodic minor scale   A minor scale that uses raised sixth and seventh notes: *fi* (raised from *fa*) and *si* (raised from *sol*). Often, these notes are raised in ascending patterns, but not in descending patterns.

melody   A logical succession of musical tones.

meter   A way of organizing rhythm.

meter signature   *See* time signature.

metronome marking   A sign that appears over the top line of the staff at the beginning of a piece or section of music that indicates the tempo. It shows the kind of note that will receive the beat and the number of beats per minute as measured by a metronome.

mezzo forte *(MEH-tsoh FOR tay)* [It.] A dynamic that indicates to sing or play medium loud. (*mf*)

mezzo piano *(MEH-tsoh pee-AH-noh)* [It.] A dynamic that indicates to sing or play medium soft. (*mp*)

mezzo voce *(MEH-tsoh VOH-cheh)* [It.] With half voice; reduced volume and tone.

minor chord   A chord that can be based on the *la, do,* and *mi* of a minor scale.

minor scale   A scale that has *la* as its home tone, or keynote. It is made up of a specific arrangement of whole steps and half steps in the following order: W + H +W + W + H + W + W.

minor tonality   A song that is based on a minor scale with *la* as its keynote, or home tone.

mixed meter   A technique in which the time signature or meter changes frequently within a piece of music.

Mixolydian scale *(mix-oh-LIH-dee-an)* [Gr.] A modal scale that starts and ends on *sol.*

modal scale   A scale based on a mode. Like major and minor scales, each modal scale is made up of a specific arrangement of whole steps and half steps, with the half steps occurring between *mi* and *fa,* and *ti* and *do.*

mode   An early system of pitch organization that was used before major and minor scales and keys were developed.

modulation   A change in the key or tonal center of a piece of music within the same song.

molto   [It.] Very or much; for example, *molto rit.* means "much slower."

motet *(moh-teht)*   Originating as a Medieval and Renaissance polyphonic song, this choral form of composition became an unaccompanied work, often in contrapuntal style. Also, a short, sacred choral piece with a Latin text that is used in religious services but is not a part of the regular mass.

motive   A shortened expression, sometimes contained within a phrase.

music critic   A writer who gives an evaluation of a musical performance.

music notation   Any means of writing down music, including the use of notes, rests and symbols.

musical   A play or film whose action and dialogue are combined with singing and dancing.

musical theater   An art form that combines acting, singing, and dancing to tell a story. It often includes staging, costumes, lighting and scenery.

mysterioso   [It.] Perform in a mysterious or haunting way; to create a haunting mood.

N

narrative song   A song that tells a story.

national anthem   A patriotic song adopted by nations through tradition or decree.

nationalism   Patriotism; pride of country. This feeling influenced many Romantic composers such as Wagner, Tchaikovsky, Dvořák, Chopin and Brahms.

natural   A symbol that cancels a previous sharp or flat, or a sharp or flat in a key signature. (♮)

natural minor scale   A minor scale that uses no altered pitches or accidentals.

no breath mark   A direction not to take a breath at a specific place in the composition. (N.B.)

non troppo (*nahn TROH-poh*)   [It.] Not too much; for example, *allegro non troppo*, "not too fast."

notation   Written notes, symbols and directions used to represent music within a composition.

O

octave   An interval of two pitches that are eight notes apart on a staff.

ode   A poem written in honor of a special person or occasion. These poems were generally dedicated to a member of a royal family. In music, an ode usually includes several sections for choir, soloists and orchestra.

opera   A combination of singing, instrumental music, dancing and drama that tells a story.

optional divisi (*opt.div.*)   Indicating a split in the music into optional harmony, shown by a smaller cued note.

oral tradition   Music that is learned through rote or by ear and is interpreted by its performer(s).

oratorio (*or-uh-TOR-ee-oh*)   [It.] A dramatic work for solo voices, chorus and orchestra presented without theatrical action. Usually, oratorios are based on a literary or religious theme.

ostinato (*ahs-tuh-NAH-toh*)   [It.] A rhythmic or melodic passage that is repeated continuosly.

overture   A piece for orchestra that serves as an introduction to an opera or other dramatic work.

P

palate   The roof of the mouth; the hard palate is at the front, the soft palate is at the back.

parallel motion   A technique in which two or more melodic lines move in the same direction.

parallel sixths   A group of intervals that are a sixth apart and which move at the same time and in the same direction.

parallel thirds   A group of intervals that are a third apart and which move at the same time and in the same direction.

part-singing   Two or more parts singing an independent melodic line at the same time.

patsch   The act of slapping one's hands on one's thighs.

pentatonic scale   A five-tone scale using the pitches *do, re, mi, sol* and *la*.

perfect fifth   An interval of two pitches that are five notes apart on a staff.

perfect fourth   An interval of two pitches that are four notes apart on a staff.

phrase   A musical idea with a beginning and an end.

Phrygian scale *(FRIH-gee-an)* [Gk.] A modal scale that starts and ends on *mi*.

pianissimo *(pee-ah-NEE-see-moh)* [It.] A dynamic that indicates to sing or play very soft. (*pp*)

piano *(pee-AH-noh)* [It.] A dynamic that indicates to sing or play soft. (*p*)

pitch Sound, the result of vibration; the highness or lowness of a tone, determined by the number of vibrations per second.

pitch matching In a choral ensemble, the ability to sing the same notes as those around you.

piu *(pew)* [It.] More; for example, *piu forte* means "more loudly."

poco *(POH-koh)* [It.] Little; for example *poco dim.* means "a little softer."

poco a poco *(POH-koh ah POH-koh)* [It.] Little by little; for example, *poco a poco cresc.* means "little by little increase in volume."

polyphony *(pah-LIH-fun-nee)* [Gk.] Literally, "many sounding." A type of music in which there are two or more different melodic lines being sung or played at the same time. Polyphony was refined during the Renaissance, and this period is sometimes called "golden age of polyphony."

polyrhythms A technique in which several different rhythms are performed at the same time.

presto *(PREH-stoh)* [It.] Very fast.

program music A descriptive style of music composed to relate or illustrate a specific incident, situation or drama; the form of the piece is often dictated or influenced by the nonmusical program. This style commonly occurs in music composed during the Romantic period.

Q

quarter note A note that represents one beat of sound when the quarter note receives the beat.

quarter rest A rest that represents one beat of silence when the quarter note receives the beat.

quartet A group of four singers or instrumentalists.

R

rallentando *(rall.)* *(rahl-en-TAHN-doh)* [It.] Meaning to "perform more and more slowly." *See* ritard.

refrain A repeated section at the end of each phrase or verse in a song. Also known as a chorus.

register, vocal A term used for different parts of the singer's range, such as head register, or head voice (high notes); and chest register, or chest voice (low notes).

relative minor scale A minor scale that shares the same key signature as its corresponding major scale. Both scales share the same half steps, between *mi* and *fa*, and *ti* and *do*.

Renaissance period The historical period in Western civilization from 1430 to 1600.

repeat sign A symbol that indicates that a section of music should be repeated. (:||)

repetition The restatement of a musical idea; repeated pitches; repeated "A" section in ABA form.

requiem *(REK-wee-ehm)* [Lt.] Literally, "rest." A mass written and performed to honor the dead and comfort the living.

resonance Reinforcement and intensification of sound by vibration.

rest A symbol used in music notation to indicate silence.

rhythm The combination of long and short notes and rests in music. These may move with the beat, faster than the beat or slower than the beat.

ritard *(rit.)* *(ree-TAHRD)* [It.] A tempo marking that indicates to gradually get slower.

Romantic period The historical period in Western civilization from 1820 to 1900.

rondo form A form in which a repeated section is separated by several contrasting sections.

rote The act of learning a song by hearing it over and over again.

round *See* canon.

rubato *(roo-BAH-toh)* [It.] The freedom to slow down and/or speed up the tempo without changing the overall pulse of a piece of music.

S

sacred music Music associated with religious services or themes.

scale A group of pitches that are sung or played in succession and are based on a particular home tone, or keynote.

scat singing An improvisational style of singing that uses nonsense syllables instead of words. It was made popular by jazz trumpeter Louis Armstrong.

sea chantey A song sung by sailors, usually in rhythm with their work.

secular music Music not associated with religious services or themes.

sempre *(SEHM-preh)* [It.] Always, continually.

sempre accelerando *(sempre accel.)* *(SEHM-preh ahk-chel)* [It.] A term that indicates to gradually increase the tempo of a piece or section of music.

sequence A successive musical pattern that begins on a higher or lower pitch each time it is repeated.

serenata [It.] A large-scale musical work written in honor of a special occasion. Generally performed in the evening or outside, it is often based on a mythological theme.

sforzando *(sfohr-TSAHN-doh)* [It.] A sudden strong accent on a note or chord. (*sfz*)

sharp A symbol that raises the pitch of a given note one half step.

shekere An African shaker consisting of a hollow gourd surrounded by beads.

sight-sing Reading and singing music at first sight.

simile *(sim.)* *(SIM-ee-leh)* [It.] To continue the same way.

simple meter Any meter in which the quarter note receives the beat, and the division of the beat is based on two eighth notes. 2/4, 3/4 and 4/4 are examples of simple meter.

singing posture The way one sits or stands while singing.

sixteenth note A note that represents one quarter beat of sound when the quarter note receives the beat. Four sixteenth notes equal one beat of sound when the quarter note receives the beat.

sixteenth rest A rest that represents one quarter beat of silence when the quarter note receives the beat. Four sixteenth rests equal one beat of silence when the quarter note receives the beat.

skipwise motion The movement from a given note to another note that is two or more notes above or below it on the staff.

slur A curved line placed over or under a group of notes to indicate that they are to be performed without a break.

solfège syllables Pitch names using *do, re, mi, fa, sol, la, ti, do,* etc.

solo One person singing or playing an instrument alone.

sonata-allegro form A large ABA form consisting of three sections: exposition, development and recapitulation. This form was made popular during the Classical period.

soprano The highest-sounding female voice.

sostenuto *(SAHS-tuh-noot-oh)* [It.] The sustaining of a tone or the slackening of tempo.

sotto voce In a quiet, subdued manner; "under" the voice.

spirito *(SPEE-ree-toh)* [It.] Spirited; for example, *con spirito* ("with spirit").

spiritual Songs that were first sung by African American slaves, usually based on biblical themes or stories.

staccato *(stah-KAH-toh)* [It.] A short and detached style of singing or playing.

staff A series of five horizontal lines and four spaces on which notes are written. A staff is like a ladder. Notes placed higher on the staff sound higher than notes placed lower on the staff.

stage presence A performer's overall appearance on stage, including enthusiasm, facial expression and posture.

staggered breathing In ensemble singing, the practice of planning breaths so that no two singers take a breath at the same time, thus creating the overall effect of continuous singing.

staggered entrances A technique in which different parts and voices enter at different times.

stanza A section in a song in which the words change on each repeat. Also known as a verse.

stepwise motion The movement from a given note to another note that is directly above or below it on the staff.

strophe A verse or stanza in a song.

strophic A form in which the melody repeats while the words change from verse to verse.

style The particular character of a musical work; often indicated by words at the beginning of a composition, telling the performer the general manner in which the piece is to be performed.

subdominant chord A chord built on the fourth note of a scale. In a major scale, this chord uses the notes *fa, la* and *do*, and it may be called the **IV** ("four") chord, since it is based on the fourth note of the major scale, or *fa*. In a minor scale, this chord uses the notes *re, fa* and *la*, and it may be called the **iv** ("four") chord, since it is based on the fourth note of the minor scale, or *re*.

subito (sub.) *(SOO-bee-toh)* [It.] Suddenly.

suspension The holding over of one or more musical tones in a chord into the following chord, producing a momentary discord.

swing rhythms Rhythms in which the second eighth note of each beat is played or sung like the last third of triplet, creating an uneven, "swing" feel. A style often found in jazz and blues. Swing rhythms are usually indicated at the beginning of a song or section.

syllabic *See* syllabic singing.

syllabic singing A style of text setting in which one syllable is sung on each note.

syllabic stress The stressing of one syllable over another.

symphonic poem A single-movement work for orchestra, inspired by a painting, play or other literary or visual work. Franz Liszt was a prominent composer of symphonic poems. Also known as a tone poem.

symphony A large-scale work for orchestra.

syncopation The placement of accents on a weak beat or a weak portion of the beat, or on a note or notes that normally do not receive extra emphasis.

synthesizer A musical instrument that produces sounds electronically, rather than by the physical vibrations of an acoustic instrument.

T

tempo   Terms in music that indicate how fast or slow to sing or play.

tempo I or tempo primo   *See* a tempo.

tenor   The highest-sounding male voice.

tenuto *(teh-NOO-toh)*   [It.] A symbol placed above or below a given note indicating that the note should receive stress and/or that its value should be slightly extended. ( )

text   Words, usually set in a poetic style, that express a central thought, idea or narrative.

texture   The thickness of the different layers of horizontal and vertical sounds.

theme   A musical idea, usually a melody.

theme and variation form   A musical form in which variations of the basic theme make up the composition.

third   An interval of two pitches that are three notes apart on a staff.

tie   A curved line used to connect two or more notes of the same pitch together in order to make one longer note.

tied notes   Two or more notes of the same pitch connected together with a tie in order to make one longer note.

timbre   The tone quality of a person's voice or musical instrument.

time signature   The set of numbers at the beginning of a piece of music. The top number indicates the number of beats per measure. The bottom number indicates the kind of note that receives the beat. Time signature is sometimes called meter signature.

to coda   Skip to (θ) or CODA.

tone color   That which distinguishes the voice or tone of one singer or instrument from another; for example, a soprano from an alto, or a flute from a clarinet. *See* timbre.

tonic chord   A chord built on the home tone, or keynote of a scale. In a major scale, this chord uses the notes *do, mi* and *sol*, and it may be called the **I** ("one") chord, since it is based on the first note of the major scale, or *do*. In a minor scale, this chord uses the notes *la, do* and *mi*, and it may be called the **i** ("one") chord, since it is based on the first note of the minor scale, or *la*.

treble clef   A clef that generally indicates notes that sound higher than middle C.

trio   A group of three singers or instrumentalists with usually one on a part.

triplet   A group of notes in which three notes of equal duration are sung in the time normally given to two notes of equal duration.

troppo *(TROHP-oh)*   [It.] Too much; for example, *allegro non troppo* ("not too fast").

tutti *(TOO-tee)*   [It.] Meaning "all" or "together."

twelve-tone music   A type of music that uses all twelve tones of the scale equally. Developed in the early twentieth century, Arnold Schoenberg is considered to be the pioneer of this style of music.

two-part music   A type of music in which two different parts are sung or played.

U

unison   All parts singing or playing the same notes at the same time.

V

variation   A modification of a musical idea, usually after its initial appearance in a piece.

vivace *(vee-VAH-chay)*   [It.] Very fast; lively.

vocal jazz   A popular style of music characterized by strong prominent meter, improvisation and dotted or syncopated patterns. Sometimes sung *a cappella*.

whole note   A note that represents four beats of sound when the quarter note receives the beat.   o

whole rest   A rest that represents four beats of silence when the quarter note receives the beat.   ▬

whole step   The combination of two successive half steps.

word painting   A technique in which the music reflects the meaning of the words.

word stress   The act of singing important parts of the text in a more accented style than the other parts.

yoik   A vocal tradition of the Sámi people of the Arctic region of Sampi that features short melodic phrases that are repeated with slight variations.

Classified Index

A Cappella

Broadway

Canon

Composers

Folk

Gospel

Instruments

Index of Songs and Spotlights

Spotlights

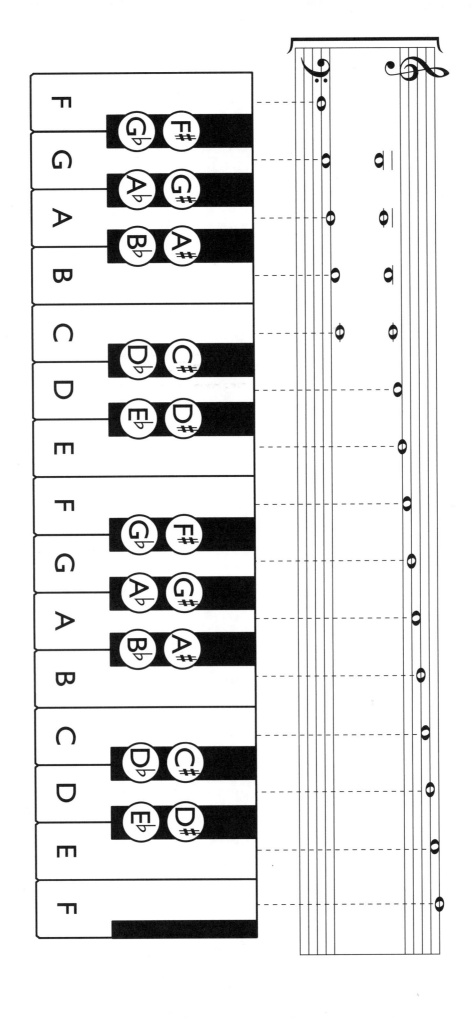